MORE
DAILY
VEG

MORE DAILY VEG

Joe Woodhouse
No fuss or frills just great vegetarian food

Kyle Books

An Hachette UK Company
www.hachette.co.uk

First published in Great Britain in 2023 by
Kyle Books, an imprint of Octopus Publishing Group
Limited
Carmelite House
50 Victoria Embankment
London EC4Y 0DZ
www.octopusbooks.co.uk
www.octopusbooksusa.com

ISBN: 9781804190845

Text copyright © Joe Woodhouse 2023
Design and layout copyright
© Octopus Publishing Group Limited 2023
Photography copyright © Joe Woodhouse 2023

Distributed in the US by Hachette Book Group,
1290 Avenue of the Americas,
4th and 5th Floors, New York, NY 10104

Distributed in Canada by Canadian Manda Group,
664 Annette St., Toronto, Ontario, Canada M6S 2C8

Publishing Director **Judith Hannam**
Publisher **Joanna Copestick**
Editorial Assistant **Emma Hanson**
Designer **Helen Bratby**
Photographer **Joe Woodhouse**
Production **Emily Noto**

A Cataloguing in Publication record for this
title is available from the British Library

Printed and bound in China

10 9 8 7 6 5 4 3 2 1

Acknowledgements

Wilfred you have helped with this book as well as the
first. It is your enthusiasm and inquisitiveness that
drives a lot of the creative process. As well as your
massive love of fennel and all things food related.

Thank you to my ever lovely wife Olia. Lots of
feedback and sitting through multiple testings of
recipes. All with encouragement and a smile.

My mother for rather direct and honest feedback.
Mostly positive!

Emily Sweet for guiding the ship in such a stable and
supportive manner. Thank you.

Everyone at Kyle Books along the whole process. It is
always such a pleasure to work with all of you. Judith
thank you for trusting in me and allowing me to do my
thing. Emma Hanson this book is so very much better
for having you work on it, thank you.

Helen Bratby for once again bringing everything to
life through sensitive and thoughtful design. Thank
you so much.

Nigella and Jeremy a brace of lovely words that
make me smile and blush with appreciation. It means
everything. Thank you.

Thank you to everyone that cooked from the first
book and enjoyed meals made from it. It is such a
massive source of energy to see the recipes coming
to life all around the globe.

Again to anyone that is in the position to share their
experience and knowledge that spends that little
extra time to help someone fully understand.

CONTENTS

Introduction

This book is about approachable and satisfying plates of food, a natural continuation to my first cookbook, *Your Daily Veg*. I have been drawing inspiration from dishes and meals that I have eaten over the years – some from my travels with work in different cultures and countries, always those that have stuck with me. Plates of food that have stood out primarily because they were so tasty. Many dishes were made up on the spot with the ingredients sitting on the board in front of me, drawing on experiences and techniques learned along the way.

The feel and basis still revolve around great produce and giving it a platform to shine. My cooking is all about championing the vegetable. I've been in two minds as to whether or not to mention suggestions for meat or fish pairings for some of the recipes within the book. As I don't want to upset or put off anyone who isn't into that, I've refrained. But the reality, and the hope, is that this book will be used by those who consume animals as well as those who don't. If it helps people to eat more vegetables – whether that be swapping out meat or fish for a few meals or just having more unusual vegetable dishes on offer to keep everyone interested – then it is better for everyone.

Exploring and eating outside of what you know are among the greatest pleasures in life. It's the magical thing that happens when you first taste and experience a new flavour – your senses tuning up and into what's going on. Hopefully there are both the familiar and some new territory for you to explore within this book. I've tried to keep ingredient lists and methods fairly simple, as well as adding as many variations or substitutions that I can think of. There are some simple dishes to ease you in as well as some slightly more involved ones.

I tend to stick a pack of beans or pulses on to soak before going to bed, then decide in the morning what to turn them into. This book is very much how we eat. Less of the fried stuff maybe, or at least reserving it for when friends are round. Instead, big piles of fresh, crunchy salads and pots of beans and lentils in sauces.

Naturally since my son has grown up bit and helps a lot more in the actual cooking, recipes and ideas have been shaped by his palate as well as mine. This book could well have been a deep dive on fennel – his favourite vegetable. Which brings me to you as the maker of these recipes. Please do use the recipes as templates. If you don't have the odd ingredient, substitutions are welcome. Or use your preference if you aren't so keen on something. Equally, if you don't have the majority of the ingredients, using the recipes as inspiration and forging your own path still gives the book purpose. Cooking and eating should be fun and food taste great to you, most importantly.

I have included quite a bit of quick pickles in this book, as I really do keep the fridge door fully stocked with various jars of pickled veg. It is such an easy way to lift a plate of food. Preserving is also great if you have too much of something or plans change and you don't want ingredients to go to waste. It takes no time at all to quickly heat up the pickling liquor. I get complaints from my family if things start to run low – especially the chillies on page 90. They go on and with pretty much everything. I also mostly make double quantities of the recipes and keep them in big jars. They add such a wonderful freshness and crunch to dishes, especially bowls of warming beans and stews.

Also I should say I don't actually peel vegetables, which is why it isn't ever a step in the recipes. That is unless the skin is so rough and knobbly it traps lots of excess dirt in it. In that case of course take it off, but otherwise there is no need. It is just a waste of food, and time, frankly. I try and use as much of the vegetable as possible. Herb stalks, if soft enough, can be chopped and added to sauces or infused in a sauce, if tougher. If you know you have a big cooking session coming up consider having a large pot to put trimmings and offcuts into, then simmer in water to make vegetable stock. I tend to cover in water, bring to a simmer for 15–20 minutes, then put a lid on the pot and turn off the heat, letting it infuse for a couple of hours. Then strain, and reduce if you want a more intense liquid.

I hope that you find inspiration from the following recipes. As I mentioned, I've tried to keep things fairly simple and accessible. But please, please do make the recipes your own. They are all fairly easy to swap elements in or out of as well as providing the basis for taking in other directions that suit you and those you are cooking for. Time spent in the kitchen should be one of the more relaxing and enjoyable parts of the day. Have fun.

POTATOES

Oh **POTATOES**, you wonderful things. Often found on our breakfast table, especially on weekends, as well as lunches and dinners – you can't really go wrong. I always cook extra whenever I'm boiling potatoes or making jacket potatoes. They are such a great platform for other flavours while not being too shabby themselves, needing only a little fat and salt to transform into something magical.

POTATO
& onion pan cake

I use a 24cm (9½in) cast iron pan for this. Everything just fits and it does shrink a fair amount while cooking. Using a larger pan means it will cook quicker and be thinner. Good either way. I've started using a sheet of parchment paper to cook the potato on, as it means that the mix doesn't stick to the pan and it is easier to turn out. It also means you can use the lower end of the oil amount. I crumple up a sheet that is larger than the pan then unravel and place in the pan. The crumpling helps it sit into the sides better. By all means cook directly in the pan, but if you're having issues with the cake sticking then it is worth trying the parchment paper. SERVES 4–6

- 800g (1lb 10oz) potatoes, I like King Edward or Maris Piper
- 2 onions, thinly sliced
- 60–100ml (2–3½fl oz) olive oil
- sea salt flakes and black pepper

1. Half fill a large mixing bowl with cold water. Then, either on the julienne attachment on a mandolin or using the grating disc on a food processor or a good old box grater, grate all the potatoes. Add to the water along with the onions. Leave for 10 minutes, then thoroughly drain. Lightly season with salt and pepper.

2. Heat a cast-iron or heavy weight frying pan over a medium heat. If using the parchment paper, add it in now. Add two-thirds of the oil, heat through. Then carefully add add the potato mix into the pan a fistful at a time. Gently pat down to fill out the bottom of the pan. Turn the heat to medium-low. Cook for 10–15 minutes until golden and crisp.

3. Place a plate over the top of the pan and carefully and swiftly invert the pan to turn out the cake. Then either reusing the parchment paper if you are using this or add the remaining oil straight into the pan. Slide the cake back in to cook the underside. Cook for a further 10–15 minutes until golden and crisp.

4. If either side isn't brown enough, flip and continue to cook some more until you are happy with the level of golden crispness. This goes well with a fried egg and mushroom ketchup from page 58.

PATATAS BRAVAS
& plant-based aioli

I wanted a quick and oven-friendly version of chips. Fondly remembering many an evening sat in a square somewhere in Spain munching on patatas bravas, it seemed a good way to go. I primarily make plant-based mayonnaise these days as it is very stable and sits happily in the fridge. Use a low-flavour oil and go strong on the mustard as this aids the emulsification. If you want a thicker mayo, add more oil; equally if it reaches a consistency you like before all the oil is in, stop there. It will firm up some more once chilled. Leave out the garlic to have straight mayo for other recipes. SERVES 6

- 800g (1lb 12oz) potatoes, such as Russet, Yukon Gold, King Edward, Maris Piper
- 100ml (3½fl oz) olive oil

FOR THE TOMATO SAUCE
- 2 tablespoons olive oil
- 2 garlic cloves, sliced
- 1 small onion, finely diced
- 1 tablespoon sweet paprika
- 1 tablespoon hot paprika
- 400g (14oz) can plum tomatoes

FOR THE PLANT-BASED AIOLI
- 100ml (3½fl oz) aquafaba (from a jar or can of chickpeas)
- 400ml (14fl oz) sunflower oil
- 2 tablespoons Dijon mustard
- 1-2 tablespoons lemon juice or vinegar
- 1 garlic clove, grated, or 1 teaspoon garlic powder
- a healthy pinch of sea salt flakes

1. Preheat the oven to 200°C (400°F), Gas Mark 6. Place a roasting tray in the oven to warm up.

2. Cut the potatoes into roughly even 3-4cm (1¼-1½in) cubes. Carefully add the oil to the tray in the oven. Allow to heat up for 2 minutes. Then remove it with care and set on a stable surface. Gently add the potatoes, tipping away from yourself so no oil splashes at you. With a spatula or tongs, turn the potatoes so they are coated in oil. Return the tray to the oven and roast the potatoes for 25 minutes. Remove the tray and turn the potatoes. Return to the oven for a further 10-15 minutes until they are evenly crisp and golden.

3. Meanwhile, in a medium saucepan heat the oil for the sauce over a medium heat. Add the garlic and onion and cook, stirring occasionally, for 8-10 minutes. Add the paprika and follow with the tomatoes. Roughly crush them to help them break down. Half-fill the can with water and add to the pan. Simmer for 10-15 minutes. Remove from the heat and blend until smooth. Set aside.

4. As the sauce cooks, either with a stick blender in a tall jug or jar that fits the blender all the way to the bottom, add the aioli ingredients and blend on high speed, holding the position at the bottom. Then slowly bring the blender up in a rocking action until all the oil is incorporated and you have a thick emulsion. Alternatively, in a blender, add all the aioli ingredients except the oil. Turn on to high speed, then trickle in the oil through the top hole until you have a thick emul-sion. Taste for salt, add more if needed and blend to incorporate.

5. Remove the potatoes from the tray to a sieve or a plate lined with kitchen paper to drain any excess oil. Sprinkle well with salt. Serve with the tomato sauce, aioli and a cold beer.

Ricotta & *POTATO* dumplings with a quick fresh tomato & olive oil sauce

These are great as a separate course in a meal or to build a lunch around, with a big salad on the side. Pushing the dimples into the dumplings means they cook more evenly and helps trap the sauce when eating. I do a test one in a small pot of water to see if they hold together and then proceed to make the rest. Freeze on a tray and then place in a container or bags so they can be on hand for a swift meal, cooked straight from the freezer in simmering water. Use the sauce from page 104 if you want to use canned tomatoes. If using smaller tomatoes there is no need to peel them. The dumplings go very well with the roast tomato and fennel on page 108 as an alternative sauce. SERVES 4-6

- 1.2kg (2lb 10oz) floury potatoes, cleaned, such as Maris Piper or King Edward
- 250g (9oz) ricotta
- 50g (1¾oz) Italian-style hard cheese or similar hard cheese, grated, plus extra to serve
- 25g (1oz) chives
- 2 eggs
- 150–200g (5⅓–7oz) 00, bread flour or plain flour

FOR THE SAUCE
- 500g (17⅔oz) tomatoes, with a cross cut into the skin at the tip of each one
- 4–6 tablespoons extra-virgin olive oil
- 3 garlic cloves, sliced
- sea salt flakes and black pepper

1. Preheat the oven to 180°C (350°F), Gas Mark 4. Place the potatoes on a baking tray and bake for 45 minutes–1 hour, depending on their size, until completely soft in the centre when pierced with a knife.

2. When cool enough to handle, cut them in half and scoop out the flesh into a bowl. Reserve the skins on the tray. Mash or pass the flesh through a ricer into a bowl. Add the ricotta and hard cheese and mix well to combine. Add a good pinch of salt, the chives and the eggs. Mix to incorporate well. Mix in the flour, then turn out onto a work surface and gently knead together to form a dough.

3. Have a bowl of water on the side to keep your fingers wet. Pinch off walnut-sized pieces and roll into balls and place them on a greased baking tray. Push each one in the centre with your index finger to form a dimple in each. Chill in the fridge or freezer if making ahead.

4. Place the tomatoes in a large mixing bowl and pour over boiling water. Wait for 15–20 seconds, then remove them with a slotted spoon to an ice bath. Allow them to chill for a couple of minutes. Pick out the tomatoes and the skins should rub off, peel any stubborn bits away. Quarter the tomatoes and cut out the seeds (reserve for another recipe or have on toast with oil for breakfast). Cut each tomato petal into strips and then cut back along to dice.

5. Heat 2 tablespoons of olive oil in a medium pan with the garlic. Once it is bubbling and aromatic, add the tomatoes with a pinch of salt. Cook for 3–5 minutes until the tomato dice is beginning to collapse. Take off the heat and check the seasoning. Add pepper and more salt if needed.

6. In a large pot of salted water, add your dumplings, in batches if needed. Don't overcrowd them. When they float to the top, allow them to cook for a minute, then remove them to a bowl with 2 tablespoons of oil and toss to coat.

7. Spoon your tomato sauce onto plates and top with the dumplings. Finish with a grind of black pepper and a drizzle of oil. More cheese never hurt.

You can also use the potato skins to make a pre-dinner snack. Toss them in 2 tablespoons of oil and lay out evenly on a baking tray. Mix the 25g (1oz) finely chopped chives with 150g (5½oz) grated cheese, such as Cheddar, and evenly distribute over the skins. Add a pinch of salt and bake in the oven for 5–7 minutes until the cheese is melted and beginning to bubble. Serve with crème fraîche or yogurt.

Urojo – Zanzibar
POTATO soup

I had this soup in a market in Zanzibar. It was one of those moments that catches you off guard. A seemingly simple potato soup, but it really is much more than the sum of its parts. So understated but it really delivers. This is my memory of the version I had. You can also add fried peanuts or a hard-boiled egg. I don't remember the soup being spicy, but you could add a chilli or two to the pot to simmer along. The roasted peanuts without salt are worth seeking out as they work really well here but are also great in salads and for general snacking. SERVES 4

- 800g (1lb 12oz) potatoes, I favour Maris Piper or King Edward, cut into 2–3cm (¾–1¼in) cubes
- 2 heaped tablespoons gram flour
- ½ teaspoon ground turmeric
- 1 red onion, finely sliced
- juice of 2 limes
- juice of 1 lemon
- sea salt flakes

TO GARNISH (optional)
- few stalks of coriander
- roasted unsalted peanuts
- sliced green chilli
- finely sliced red onion
- wedges of lemon and lime

1. Place the potatoes, a good pinch of salt and 1 litre (1¾ pints) of water in a pan. Bring to a simmer.

2. After 5 minutes, in a small bowl, whisk the flour and the turmeric with a cup of the cooking water until smooth. Add it to the pan. Add the red onion with the citrus juices. Cook for 7–10 minutes until the potato is tender and the broth has thickened slightly.

3. Taste and add more salt if needed. Serve in bowls with any toppings you like alongside for people to add themselves.

POTATO & tomato frittata

I was on holiday in a cabin in the woods of central Belgium, with my three year old and my wife. We'd stocked up on produce from a brilliant market in Brussels. I knew we would be out the whole day and needed a picnic lunch, so I quickly made this frittata in the morning, cut it into sections and took it with us. Some grated cheese that melts well added before the pan goes in the oven either in, on top, or both is most welcome. Really ripe, full-flavoured tomatoes make the dish. SERVES 6

- 4 tablespoons olive oil
- 400g (14oz) tomatoes, roughly diced into 3-4cm (1¼-1½in) cubes
- 500g (1lb 2oz) cooked potatoes, any variety works, I lean toward Maris Piper or King Edward, cut into 3-4cm (1¼-1½in) cubes
- 10g (¼oz) tarragon, leaves picked
- 8 eggs, beaten
- sea salt flakes and black pepper

1. Preheat the oven to 180°C (350°F), Gas Mark 4. Add the oil to a large, ovenproof frying pan over a medium-high heat. Follow with the tomatoes and a good pinch of salt. Cook for 2-3 minutes to warm through and drive out some moisture. Add the potatoes and cook for 2-3 minutes to warm them through.

2. Mix the tarragon and a few good grinds of black pepper with the eggs and pour it into the pan. Turn the heat to medium. Give everything a good mix to distribute the egg. Make sure the tomatoes and potatoes are evenly distributed about the pan. Place the pan in the oven to cook for 15 minutes. Rotate it the best you can and continue to cook for a further 10-15 minutes until the centre is set and the top is golden.

3. Remove from the oven. Using an ovenproof glove or tea towel, set on the hob to cool slighting. The frittata can be served straight from the pan. Or if you allow it to cool for 5-10 minutes it should shrink back slightly and be easier to remove from the pan. Slide it onto a serving plate or chopping board.

POTATO, green & white bean pesto salad

A riff on the Ligurian pasta dish with trofie, this time using beans to make more of a salad. I love the flavour combination and the white beans add an extra creaminess. I use walnuts as it adds a different dimension, but almonds would also work so do play with using other nuts. You can also add trofie or other small pasta shapes to make into a main.

SERVES 4 AS A STARTER OR SIDE

- 500g (1lb 2oz) new potatoes, cleaned
- 100g (3½oz) walnut halves
- 125ml (4½fl oz) extra-virgin olive oil
- 60g (2¼oz) hard sheep's cheese or Italian-style hard cheese, finely grated
- 2 lemons: zest and juice of 1, 1 sliced

TO SERVE
- 100g (3½oz) basil
- 400g (14oz) fine green beans, tough stalks removed
- 660g (1lb 7½oz) jar of white beans such as cannellini, haricot or butter beans, or 2 x 400g (14oz) tins would also work
- sea salt flakes and black pepper

1. Preheat the oven to 180°C (350°F), Gas Mark 4. Cut any larger potatoes in half so they are all roughly the same size. Bring the potatoes to a simmer in a pan of well-salted water. Make sure the saucepan will fit the green beans as well.

2. Toast the walnuts in the oven at 200°C (400°F), Gas Mark 6 for 8–12 minutes until just golden. Leave to cool slightly. Then add to a blender with the olive oil, cheese, lemon zest and juice and most of the basil, reserving a few leaves to serve. Blitz until combined; don't go too crazy, some texture is good.

3. When a knife nearly goes through the potatoes, add the green beans and cook for 5 minutes. You may need to top up with boiling water first.

4. Drain and rinse the white beans. Add to a mixing bowl with the pesto. Drain and rinse the potatoes and green beans briefly under cold water to refresh slightly. Add to the bowl and toss everything to combine. Add a good grind of coarse black pepper, the reserved basil leaves and serve with the lemon slices alongside.

Warm *POTATO* salad with Szechuan pepper

This potato salad is happy alongside noodles dressed in chilli oil or topped with a fried egg and chives as a lighter meal. I fell in love with this dish eating it at Chinese restaurants. The just-cooked crunchy potatoes, vinegar freshness and satisfying tingle of the Szechuan pepper are extremely addictive. A while back I saw pineapple vinegar on the shelf in a Vietnamese shop, a revelation. If you can find it, it works very well here, or as a substitute for rice vinegar in other dishes. Finely sliced spring onions can go in right at the end, as well as toasted sesame seeds. SERVES 4 AS A SIDE

- 600g (1lb 5oz) potatoes, I prefer waxy, such as Charlotte or Anya, as the strands stay more separate
- 3 tablespoons neutral oil, such as groundnut or sunflower
- 1 heaped teaspoon Szechuan peppercorns, roughly crushed
- 1 heaped teaspoon chilli flakes
- 3 tablespoons rice vinegar or pineapple vinegar, plus extra to taste
- sea salt flakes

1. Ideally slice the potatoes into matchsticks on a mandolin. If you don't have one, slice off a thin strip of each potato, then roll onto the flat side, and slice as thinly and evenly as possible. Then lay out the slices in an overlapping line and cut across to form matchsticks.

2. Soak the potato matchsticks in slightly salted water for 5 minutes or so to rinse off some of the starch. The potatoes can stay like this until ready to cook. When you are ready, drain well.

3. Heat the oil over a high heat in a wok or a heavy-based pan. Add the Szechuan pepper and chilli flakes, stir for 30 seconds, then add the potato. Toss everything together to combine well and cook for 7–10 minutes so the potatoes cook through but still retain a crisp bite.

4. Turn off the heat and dress in the vinegar to taste. Adjust for salt and serve.

Tel Aviv baked
SWEET POTATO
with crème fraîche,
grey salt & pink onions

Deceptively simple but a knockout flavour combination. I had this in the restaurant Port Sa'id in Tel Aviv. Sweet potatoes cooked in the oven until sticky and tender inside and the skins were crispy and papery, tempered with creamy, slightly sour crème fraîche and a good sprinkle of wet grey salt. Absolute heaven, everything in such balance. For me it was a big food moment – the guts of just serving what was basically a baked potato in this way. It has stuck with me over the years and I have recreated or paid homage in various ways. I like adding the pink pickled onions and giving the potatoes a bit of an extra char. They also work well cooked on the barbecue wrapped in foil. SERVES 6

- 6 sweet potatoes
- 100ml (3½fl oz) red wine vinegar
- 4 small red onions, finely sliced
- 200g (7oz) crème fraîche
- grey salt or sea salt flakes
- extra-virgin olive oil

1. Preheat the oven to 200°C (400°F), Gas Mark 6. Wet each potato and rub really well with your hands to dislodge any sandy soil. Rinse under running water. Then place the potatoes carefully on the oven rack and bake for 25 minutes. Turn them over and bake for a further 25 minutes until collapsed and tender inside and the skins are dry and peppery to the touch.

2. In a small pan, heat the vinegar with 100ml (3½fl oz) of water and a good pinch of salt. Pour over the sliced red onion in a small bowl. Push the onion down to submerge if necessary and allow to infuse with the vinegar and become pink.

3. Once the potatoes are nearly cooked, heat a griddle pan or cast-iron frying pan. Add the potatoes in whichever configuration is best. Batches are also fine. Cook until charred on one side, then flip and cook on the opposite side until charred.

4. Cut each potato down the middle and part a little. Divide the crème fraîche among them. Sprinkle with grey salt. Serve with the drained onions, extra salt and a drizzle of olive oil, if you like.

POTATO
& rosemary focaccia

This works fine without any toppings, or equally with whatever toppings you wish. Do push the potatoes well into the dough so they become part of it. Time is your friend here really. Try to give yourself enough space before you need the cooked bread to let the dough sit and do its thing. Although, that said, you can go one of two routes when making. If you are in a rush, just mix up the complete ingredients into a dough without doing the starter step. I like doing the starter as it brings a better fermentation and flavour as you are building up the yeast. This is essentially a fancy chip butty with the potatoes going crispy in the oven. A sprinkle of vinegar and you are complete! SERVES 12

- – 4g (⅛oz) fast action dried yeast
- – 5g (⅛oz) honey or sugar
- – 600g (1lb 5oz) unbleached white or light brown plain flour, any flour works but try to use high protein flour
- – 15g (½oz) sea salt flakes, plus extra for sprinkling
- – 125ml (4½fl oz) extra-virgin olive oil
- – 400g (14oz) potatoes, boiled until tender, any variety works, I lean toward waxier varieties such as Charlotte, Anya or Jersey Royals
- – 3 good sprigs of rosemary, leaves picked and rubbed with oil

1. In a bowl with enough room for the starter to triple in size, mix 300ml (10½fl oz) of water with the yeast and honey. Add 300g (10½oz) of the flour. Mix well to combine and cover; I use a plate. Leave out on the work surface for 1 hour. Then refrigerate for 16–24 hours.

2. The next day, add the remaining flour and starter to the bowl of a stand mixer fitted with the dough hook. In a jug, dissolve the salt in 180ml (6fl oz) of room temperature water. Start mixing on the slowest setting, gently pouring in a few tablespoons of the water at a time. Once half the water has been added, increase the speed to medium. Continue adding the water in stages, waiting until it is absorbed before adding more. Knead for a further 5 minutes.

3. Pour in 50ml (1¾fl oz) of the oil in the same fashion as the water. Keep kneading the dough for a further 5 minutes until it is smooth and doesn't break when you stretch it. Cover and leave to rest for 1 hour. Put a hand in and under one side of the dough, then let it fold back over itself. Rotate the bowl 90 degrees and repeat a further 3 times. Leave for another hour. Repeat the folding action and leave for a further hour.

4. Line your baking tray with baking parchment and add 40ml (1½fl oz) of the oil. Tip the dough into the tray. Fold each of the four sides into the middle to form a rough rectangle. Flip it back over so the top is facing up. Leave for another 1–2 hours. I cover it with a larger roasting tin turned upside down. The dough should be wobbly and pillowy. If it isn't, it needs another hour.

5. Preheat the oven to 200°C (400°F), Gas Mark 6 until properly hot. Crumble the potatoes, mix with the rosemary and scatter evenly over the dough. Mix the remaining oil with 35ml (1⅓fl oz) water and rub some on your fingers. As if you were playing the piano in a comedy fashion, push down into the dough, taking bits of potato with you all the way down the dough to redistribute the air bubbles. Pour over the remaining oil and water mixture and sprinkle with sea salt flakes. Bake for 25 minutes, rotate 180 degrees, then bake for a further 10–15 minutes until golden and risen, or the internal temperature, measured with a thermometer, is 93°C (199°F) or above.

6. Remove from the tray carefully as the oil will be hot and leave to cool on a wire rack. I pour any oil from the tray over the top to be absorbed.

POTATO
& beetroot salad

This salad is very obviously influenced by my Ukrainian wife, as well as holidays in Spain eating tapas. It is kind of a mix of the two. This version, my version, came about when I was making it once. In autopilot mode I cooked the onions rather than leaving them raw but I really enjoy the different dimension the cooked onion gives, which shows how recipes evolve over time. I also serve mine with hard-boiled eggs to round it out to a complete meal. I have a lot of time for recipes that you can make ahead and pull out when needed. To have a nutritious and flavourful meal ready to go is not to be underrated. It also makes a good amount for a party and sits well in the fridge, so you can make it ahead. If you wanted to go down the more Ukranian route of vinegret, dress with unrefined sunflower oil and vinegar. SERVES 6 AS A SMALL STARTER, SIDE OR LIGHT LUNCH

- 500g (1lb 2oz) beetroot
- 500g (1lb 2oz) potatoes, use what you have, I lean toward Maris Piper or King Edward
- 200g (7oz) carrots, tops removed, cut into 1cm (½in) dice
- 250g (12oz) petit pois
- 2 small onions, diced
- 2 tablespoons olive oil
- 180g (6oz) mayonnaise (see page 12 for homemade)
- handful of gherkins or cornichons, diced
- sea salt flakes and black pepper
- hard-boiled eggs, to serve (optional)

1. Boil the beetroot in a pan of well-salted water until they fall off a knife when pierced. Drain and refresh under cold water. Allow them to cool.

2. In salted water boil the potatoes until they fall off a knife when pierced. Drain and allow to cool.

3. Add the carrots to a pan with just enough water to cover them. Bring to a simmer and cook for 5–7 minutes until tender. When they are done, stir in the peas. Cook for a minute, then drain and refresh under cold water.

4. Meanwhile, add the onions to a pan with the oil over a medium heat and cook for 10–12 minutes until soft but without much colour.

5. Remove the beetroot from the water and peel off the skins. Cut them into 1cm (½in) dice and add to a large mixing bowl. Dice the potatoes in a similar fashion. Add them to the mixing bowl with the carrots, peas and onions. Mix in the mayonnaise and the gherkins. Taste and add more gherkins, black pepper and more salt if needed.

6. Serve as part of a meal or as a light lunch with hard-boiled eggs, if you like.

CELERIAC BEETROOT & SQUASH

CELERIAC is a really lovely vegetable that can be the main role or the supporting act. Celeriac works really well with other flavours and has a gentle but present place on the plate. Another one that is a welcome addition to chunky soups and stews. Try it simply roasted and use as a sandwich filler.

CELERIAC remoulade

I love celeriac remoulade. Straight remoulade sandwiches are a thing, well at least to me they are. This is a dish that reminds me so strongly of travels in France, whether it is having it as a starter in a bistro in Paris, or as part of a picnic sitting by a lake in the Jura. I switch between fondness for really thin strands of celeriac and slightly chunkier ones which add a bit more texture to the final dish, like here. Go for whichever pleases you. SERVES 4–6

- 100g (3½oz) crème fraîche
- 100g (3½oz) mayonnaise (see page 12 for homemade plant-based version)
- 50g (1¾oz) Dijon mustard
- 60ml (2¼fl oz) lemon juice (about 2 lemons)
- 800g (1lb 12oz) celeriac, peeled
- sea salt flakes

    TO SERVE
- 80g (2¾oz) hazelnuts
- extra-virgin olive oil, to serve
- crusty bread

1. In a large mixing bowl, combine the crème fraîche, mayo, mustard and half the lemon juice with a large pinch of salt.

2. I like to use a mandolin with the julienne attachment set in place to slice the celeriac. However, you can easily achieve similar by slicing as evenly and as thinly as possible across the celeriac. Then stack up a few slices and repeat the action once more across the stack to form lots of little batons.

3. Toss the strands of celeriac in with the dressing as you go and mix to coat well. Once all the celeriac is in, taste for salt and lemon juice levels. Adjust accordingly.

4. It does benefit from sitting for a while. The salt and acid in the dressing help the celeriac relax and the flavours get to know one another. It keeps well for a couple of days in the fridge.

5. Preheat the oven to 180°C (350°F), Gas Mark 4. Toast the hazelnuts for 8–12 minutes until golden and then lightly crush.

6. Serve the remoulade with the lightly crushed hazelnuts and a drizzle of oil. Crusty bread is a must really.

Whole baked *CELERIAC* with herb oil & butter beans

This is a good dish to make while the oven is on in the anticipation of a meal ahead, like a Sunday lunch. If the oven is going to be on, you may as well stick the celeriac in to use some of the heat. This dish is light but it still has enough about it to satisfy. It can be made ahead and reheated when needed. If the oil isn't draining, strain it through a sieve to remove most of the solids and then retry using coffee filter paper. Using a double layer of muslin is best really. Extra-virgin olive oil works fine if you want to skip the herb oil. SERVES 4

- 50g (1¾oz) soft herbs, such as parsley, dill, chervil and coriander
- 150ml (5½fl oz) neutral oil, wwwl use sunflower
- 2 celeriac, roughly 800g (1lb 10oz) each, washed
- 2 tablespoons olive oil
- 2 onions, sliced
- 1 litre (1¾ pints) vegetable stock
- 660g (1lb 7½oz) jar butter beans or other white beans, drained, 2 x 400g (14oz) tins also work or 350g (12⅓oz) dried beans soaked in water and cooked until tender
- sea salt flakes and black pepper

1. The night or morning before, start making the herb oil. Bring a pan of salted water to a rolling boil, then add the herbs for 10 seconds. Remove into an ice bath and chill well. Drain and squeeze out most of the moisture. Add to a small blender with the neutral oil and blitz until the colour changes from milky to a darker green. Don't go too far past this point as it will take forever to separate through the coffee filter.

2. Add the oil to a double layer of muslin or a coffee filter paper, lining a funnel over the bottle or jug you wish to collect it in. I go direct into a squeezy bottle. Allow to drip slowly for 4–6 hours or overnight. Seal and keep in the fridge for up to a week.

3. Preheat the oven to 180°C (350°F), Gas Mark 4. It can be higher if you are using the oven for something else if this is a side project. Add the celeriac and cook for 1–2 hours until soft. I give them a squeeze to check – when they easily yield, they are good to go.

4. Heat the olive oil in a medium pan and cook the onion over a medium heat for 10–12 minutes until soft. Add the stock and beans with their juice. Bring to a bubble and allow to cook for 10 minutes to so the flavours get to know each other.

5. Remove the celeriac from the oven and allow to cool enough for you to peel them. I break them in half and just peel away the skin. Then break the flesh into rough chunks as you add it to the beans. Bring back to a simmer with a good pinch of salt. Taste and add more salt if needed, with some black pepper. Serve in bowls with the herb oil drizzled over.

CELERIAC puff pie

This is a reimagined version of a pie I had at the restaurant 40 Maltby Street in London. The head chef Steve Williams is the master at crafting imaginative and outrageously tasty plates of food. This was so good the first time that I returned later the same week so I could eat the pie again before it went off the menu. I've tried to make it as easy as possible to cook at home. A slightly sour cheese is a good option as a foil to the sweet notes from the squash. Or try something a little funky, like a washed rind cheese. This pie is brilliant for feeding a crowd and I like to serve it with some watercress and English mustard to cut through the richness. SERVES 8

- 300g (10½oz) deseeded squash, onion, crown prince, acorn, butternut all work fine
- 700g (1lb 7oz) peeled celeriac (about 1kg/2lb 4oz unpeeled weight)
- 3 onions, peeled sliced
- 3–4 tablespoons olive oil
- couple of sprigs of thyme, leaves picked and roughly chopped
- 2 x 325g (11½oz) sheets of puff pastry
- 300g (10½oz) cheese, coarsely grated or sliced
- 1 egg, beaten with 1 tablespoon milk
- sea salt flakes and black pepper

1. Preheat the oven to 180°C (350°F), Gas Mark 4. Line a baking dish that is smaller than one of the sheets of puff pastry by at least 3–4cm (1¼–1½in) all the way around with parchment paper. I use a 22 x 28cm (8½ x 11in) tin.

2. Slice the squash and celeriac as thinly and evenly as possible. I use a mandolin for this, but a knife is fine. Just try to keep the slices as uniform as possible. Toss the onions, squash and celeriac with the oil and thyme leaves. Season well with salt and pepper. Arrange evenly in the baking dish, ensuring that the layers are as even as possible. Bake for 30–40 minutes until a knife easily pierces through. Set aside to cool.

3. When ready to assemble, lay out one of the sheets of puff pastry on a lined baking tray. If you can, freeze this as it is. This will help with repositioning the celeriac if you miss the middle in the flip.

4. With a swift motion, invert the baking dish with the celeriac onto the centre of the puff pastry sheet. Remove the tray and the lining paper. Gently and with a definite movement, adjust the celeriac if needed. Add the cheese on top, followed by the second puff pastry sheet. Tuck the sides down around the celeriac. Then fold the bottom sheet excess back over toward the centre to form a seal. You can crimp this with your fingers or a fork if you like, then brush all over with egg wash. Bake for 30–40 minutes until the pastry is risen and golden. It is usually worth rotating the pie 180 degrees after 25 minutes to help combat hot spots in the oven.

5. Serve with salad or sides of your choosing. It's also great as it is with just a dollop of your preferred mustard .

CELERIAC soup topped with mushrooms & grains cooked in garlic butter

Elevating a simple puréed soup with different toppings is a favourite of mine. Often it is me and my wife both working from home, so I tend to make quick lunches. Soups are great for that, especially for a speedy reheating option. Adding the grains and the mushrooms makes it a bit heartier and takes it a step on from a plain bowl of soup. SERVES 6

- 3 tablespoons olive oil
- 2 onions, roughly diced
- 1 fennel bulb, woody stalks removed, roughly diced
- 2 leeks, trimmed, cleaned, whites roughly sliced, greens shredded
- 2 celeriac, roughly 800g (1lb 10oz) each, washed
- sea salt flakes

FOR THE TOPPING
- 125g (4½oz) unsalted butter
- 1 onion, diced
- 2-4 garlic cloves, finely chopped or grated
- 300g (10½oz) chestnut mushrooms, quartered
- 25g (1oz) parsley, finely chopped
- 250g (9oz) cooked grains, such as emmer, spelt, oat groats, barley
- extra-virgin olive oil, for finishing

1. Heat the oil in a large pan and add the onions and fennel over a medium heat with a good pinch of salt. Cook for 10 minutes and then add the leeks. Cook for a further 5 minutes and then add 1 litre (1¾ pints) of water and bring to a simmer.

2. Peel the celeriac by cutting off the tough outer skin. Some isn't an issue, but the main aim is to remove the root ends where lots of soil gets trapped. Roughly cube the celeriac and add to the pan. Cook for 15-20 minutes until the celeriac is completely soft.

3. Blend the soup to a smooth purée. Add more water if you think it needs it. I like my puréed soups fairly thick, so the topping should sit easily on it.

4. Meanwhile, in a large frying pan, melt the butter and add the onion with a pinch of salt. Cook for 10-12 minutes until soft and starting to colour. Add the garlic and mushrooms and cook for 4-6 minutes until the mushrooms are soft and with good colour. Add the parsley and grains and stir until warmed through.

5. Serve the soup in bowls with the mushroom grain mix on top, plus a final drizzle of good oil if you like.

When boiling **BEETROOT**, I tend to put them on to cook first thing when I come down, especially if they are older as they will take longer. This way they will be ready for when I need them later. If you are around for the morning just stick them on and set a timer to check them occasionally. Once they are done you get rewarded with their deep flavour and sweetness.

BEETROOT borani

This Iranian dish used to be on the menu when I worked at Towpath Café. I love it. Earthy beetroot lifted with yogurt and a touch of vinegar, the toppings adding extra dimensions. It was one of the first things I made for my son when he started eating solid food. I grate the cooked beetroot for him, as it adds more texture – the same ratios but equally as good. It works well as a side dish this way. It can be a dip or a cooling first course. SERVES 4

- 1kg (2lb 4oz) beetroot
- 100g (3½oz) walnut halves
- 250–350g (9–12oz) natural yogurt
- 1–2 tablespoons white wine vinegar
- 100g (3½oz) feta, roughly broken into chunks
- bunch of dill, leaves picked
- sea salt flakes
- extra-virgin olive oil or confit garlic oil (see page 64), to serve

1. Trim the tops off the beetroot. Add them to a saucepan and cover with water. Add a decent pinch of salt and bring to a simmer. Add a lid and cook for 1–2 hours until they fall off a knife when pierced. Top up the water when needed.

2. Preheat the oven to 200°C (400°F), Gas Mark 6. Toast the walnuts for 8–12 minutes until golden. Once the beetroot are done, drain them and refill the pan with cold water. Let them sit until you can handle them easily. Slip off the skins and add to a food processor. Keep one back.

3. Add the yogurt, 1 tablespoon of the vinegar and a good pinch of salt to the blender and blitz until very smooth. If too thick, add more yogurt. Taste and add more vinegar and salt according to taste. Chill in the fridge for 2–3 hours until you are ready to serve – overnight is ideal to let the flavours marry.

4. Dice the reserved beetroot into neat 1cm (½in) cubes.

5. Divide the borani between four bowls. Top with the diced beetroot, feta, walnuts and dill. Add a drizzle of oil and eat with some crusty bread.

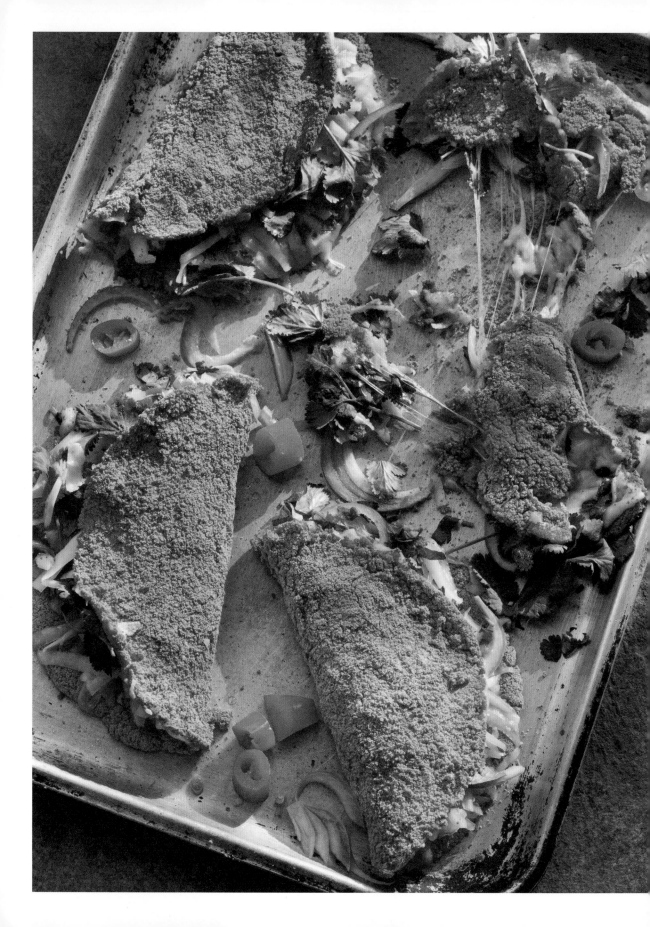

BEETROOT tapiocas

This is one of the first things I made for my wife when we were getting to know each other. I had just returned from working in Brazil and had been introduced to tapiocas, a Brazilian breakfast or snacking staple. I was instantly hooked, especially when I learned that you could use other liquids besides water to impart colour and flavour. So, coconut water, fruit and vegetable juices for instance. Have a play but don't use dairy. Traditionally, tapiocas are made plain with water, filled with cheese and served with hot sauce on the side. By all means make plain ones as a reference point. You can make a chilli sauce by blitzing the pickled chillies from page 90 to a paste. Once made, the mixture is stable in a fridge for 48 hours or so, so it can easily be prepared the night before. I use a 20cm (8in) cast-iron tapioca pan but a heavy-based frying pan of the same size will work fine. I juice beetroots and ginger to get the juice, but it is also possible to buy. MAKES 8

- 1 red onion, finely sliced
- juice of 2 limes
- 200ml (7fl oz) beetroot and ginger juice
- 400g (14oz) tapioca starch/flour
- 175g (6oz) goat Cheddar, coarsely grated, plus extra to taste
- bunch of coriander
- sea salt flakes
- hot sauce, to serve

1. First, mix the red onion with the lime juice and a pinch of salt. Set aside to macerate. This can sit in the fridge until you are ready to use it. A few days is fine.

2. Mix the beetroot and ginger juice into the flour a couple of tablespoons at a time. Run the mixture between your fingers each time to form a rough crumble, as if you were making pastry. Repeat until all the liquid is in. Then place in batches in a sieve over a fresh bowl and push the mixture through the sieve with the back of a spoon. Little 'pearls' will collect in the bowl below. The mixture is now ready to be used, or store covered in the fridge. It is good for a couple of days.

3. Once ready to cook, heat a cast-iron pan or heavy-based frying pan over a medium–low heat. Add 2–3 heaped spoonfuls of mixture into the pan and evenly spread out over the pan with the back of the spoon. Fill any gaps with a little extra mix if needed.

4. Cook gently for 1–2 minutes until set and the tapioca can be lifted free of the pan in one piece. Flip and cook for a final minute or so. This is when you can add the cheese to encourage it to melt. Fold the tapioca in half onto itself. Cook for a few more moments each side to help the cheese continue to yield. Then remove to a plate. Repeat for the rest of the mix.

5. Add some drained red onion and a few leaves of coriander. Serve with hot sauce, pickled chillies from page 90 or chilli-based condiment of your choosing alongside.

BEETROOT & kefir puree with spelt & toasted walnuts

I'm aware this is similar to the borani, but I wanted to show a different way of using a similar process. I often make beetroot purée and use as a salad dressing for leaves. I really like making a flavourful and balanced sauce that coats and brings everything together. The earthiness of the beetroot with the sourness from the yogurt or kefir is a brilliant match. Adding some blue cheese like a Stilton crumbled into the topping is a nice upgrade. Other varieties of beetroot work well also. This is a good dish if you have a few beetroot, say in a veg box, and you need to do something with them. SERVES 4

- 400g (14oz) beetroot, any colour or type, a mix also works
- 100g (3½oz) walnut halves, other nuts work well
- 150-250ml (5½-9fl oz) kefir, yogurt also works
- 400g (14oz) cooked spelt, barley or oat groats, 200g (7oz) dried should make this
- 2 spring or salad onions, finely sliced
- 20g (¾oz) chives, finely chopped
- 2 tablespoons cider vinegar
- 2 tablespoons extra-virgin olive oil
- sea salt flakes

1. Cover the beetroot in a pan with water and a good pinch of salt. Bring to a simmer with the lid on. Cook for 1-2 hours until they fall from a knife when pierced. Drain and leave to cool.

2. Preheat the oven to 180°C (350°F), Gas Mark 4. Toast the walnuts for 8-12 minutes until golden and aromatic.

3. Once cool enough to handle, rub the skins from the beetroot then trim a couple into squares and cut into a rough 1cm (½in) dice. Put the offcuts (which should be about half-two thirds of the total beetroot) into a blender with a pinch of salt and the kefir. Use enough kefir to get the purée just wet enough to blend. It wants to hold its shape on the plate, so be careful not to let it down too much.

4. Mix the diced beetroot with the grains, spring onion, chives and walnuts. Season with salt, vinegar and oil. Add more vinegar or oil if it needs it.

5. Serve the purée spooned onto plates or a platter, then the beetroot and grain mixture spooned over the top.

Diced and thrown into a pan with some onion and garlic to make pasta or roasted to sweet, caramelized perfection, **SQUASH** are in many ways the shining light of the winter months. They benefit from being left out as ornaments, getting sweeter over time. I tend to cut sections off as and when I need them, rather than using the whole beast in one go. Just wrap the cut side or lay it cut-side down on a plate and store in the fridge.

Tempura *SQUASH*

I will use any excuse to make these really as they are brilliant. I love the way the squash is just cooked inside and you have the crunchy, crispy exterior. You can make these into more of a meal by serving them in bowls with rice and pickles, or with udon noodles and broth. Equally they are perfect as a pre-dinner nibble or snack as people arrive. Use the method for other veg like broccoli, aubergine, peppers, mushrooms and sweet potato. SERVES 4-6 AS A SIDE OR CANAPÉ

- 1 onion (red kuri) squash or similar, cut ¾–1cm (⅓–½in) thick
- about 1.5–2 litres (2⅔–3½ pints) neutral oil, I use sunflower, groundnut or grape seed also work well
- 100g (3½oz) plain flour
- 100g (3½oz) cornflour
- 150–200ml (5½–7fl oz) cold sparkling water
- sea salt flakes

FOR THE DIPPING SAUCE
- 2 tablespoons soy sauce, I use an all-purpose organic soy sauce, either light or dark or a blend of both work
- 2 tablespoons rice vinegar
- 1 teaspoon honey
- small knob of fresh root ginger, peeled and finely grated

1. Mix the dipping sauce ingredients together. Taste and add any of the elements to balance it to your liking. Set aside.

2. Halve the squash, scoop out the seeds and remove the stalk. I then use a mandolin to finely slice the squash but cutting thinly with a knife works fine. Just make sure the slices are fairly even in size so the cook time is the same for all of them.

3. In a large, high-sided pan or deep-fat fryer, heat the oil to 180°C (350°F). Then gently mix 50g (1¾oz) of the plain flour with the cornflour, followed by the sparkling water until you get a fluid batter that still clings well. Don't overwork the batter as the gluten will develop too much and it will be chewy rather than crisp.

4. Working in batches, dust the squash with the remaining flour. Dip the squash slices in the batter and then carefully drop into the oil. Fry for 2–3 minutes until the batter is crisp and golden and the squash is tender. Remove to a plate lined with kitchen paper to drain and sprinkle with salt.

Whole baked baby *SQUASH* with Cheddar, cream & oats

When visiting to help pick apples at Wilding Cider, run by Beccy and Sam Leach, in Chew Magna, North Somerset, Sam made this vegetarian dish for our supper. The pair used to run the wonderful restaurant Birch in Bristol before setting their sights on cider making. Let me tell you, this simple but warming dish is a perfect foil to coming in from a cold and drizzly day in an orchard. We sat in the barn swapping ciders and wines for everyone to taste with a roaring fire going in the wood burner. A rather splendid evening. I added the green sauce to cut the richness a bit, but to be honest if you get a good-quality sharp Cheddar, it doesn't need it. SERVES 4

- 1–1.2kg (2lb 4oz–2lb 10oz) onion (red kuri) squash (about 2 squash)
- 200g (7oz) Cheddar, coarsely grated
- 200g (7oz) crème fraîche
- 100g (3½oz) rolled oats
- 2 tablespoons olive oil
- sea salt flakes and black pepper

FOR THE GREEN SAUCE
- 20g (¾oz) capers
- 50g (1¾oz) parsley
- 40g (1½oz) gherkins or cornichons
- 100–125ml (3½–4½fl oz) olive oil

1. Preheat the oven to 200°C (400°F), Gas Mark 6. With a small knife, cut the tops off the squash in a circular motion to form caps. Scoop out and compost the seeds.

2. Mix together the cheese, crème fraîche and oats, and add a good couple of pinches of salt and a healthy few grinds of black pepper.

3. Fill the squash with the oat mixture. Replace their lids. Rub each all over with a tablespoon of oil, place on a tray and bake for 25–35 minutes until a knife pierces the flesh easily.

4. Meanwhile, blend all the sauce ingredients together with salt and pepper. For a coarser sauce, hand chop everything and mix with the oil, which is equally as good, if not better.

5. Serve the squash with a salad, maybe a few potatoes to make it into a main. Add the sauce on the side and a good bottle of cider, from Wilding preferably!

Roast *SQUASH*, cavolo nero & white bean stew

Another favourite go-to for a hearty meal that won't leave you wanting a nap afterward. Beans are great. Beans in any shape or form. Creamy and comforting, they provide such a brilliant platform for flavours. This is a lovely weekend lunch that can come together fairly quickly. All the elements can be prepped ahead and then just finished when you need it, gently reheating the beans and adding in the already roasted squash and the greens to wilt. SERVES 6

- 800g (1lb 12oz) squash or pumpkin, onion, crown prince, acorn, butternut all work fine
- 6 tablespoons olive oil
- 2 onions, sliced
- 2 celery sticks, sliced
- 2 bay leaves
- 2 garlic cloves, sliced
- 1 litre (1¾ pints) vegetable stock
- 2 x 660g (1lb 7½oz) jars of white beans, canellini, haricot, butter bean all work well, or 3 x 400g (14oz) tins or 350g (12oz) dried beans soaked in water and cooked until tender
- 300g (10½oz) cavolo nero, roughly chopped and tough stalks removed
- sea salt flakes
- good extra-virgin olive oil, to serve

1. Preheat the oven to 200°C (400°F), Gas Mark 6. Halve the squash, scoop out the seeds and remove the stalk. Cut roughly into 4–5cm (1½–2in) chunks. Toss with 3 tablespoons of oil, place on a baking tray and roast for 25–35 minutes until soft and caramelized.

2. Meanwhile, in a medium pan heat the remaining oil over a medium heat and add the onions and celery with a pinch of salt. Cook for 5 minutes, then add the bay leaves and garlic and cook for a further 10 minutes until completely soft. Add the stock to the pan and bring to a simmer. Add the beans with their liquor, along with the cavolo nero, and bring to a bubble. Cook for 5–7 minutes until the cavolo nero is just starting to wilt.

3. Serve in bowls with a drizzle of good oil. Some grated hard cheese wouldn't be out of place and chunks of crusty bread to mop up any juices.

PUMPKIN & ginger rice with coriander & jalapeños

I made this once by combining cooked rice and a pumpkin soup I had made. It worked so well that I thought it deserved being a recipe in its own right. Really nourishing and bright, the silky smooth pumpkin and rice mixture is wonderfully restorative. I went simple with chilli and coriander toppings, but do use whatever you like. A good grating of hard goat's cheese wouldn't go amiss. SERVES 6

- 800g (1lb 12oz) pumpkin, squash also work fine, crown prince works particularly well
- 5 tablespoons olive oil
- 300g (10½oz) short-grain brown rice
- 2 onions, diced
- 1 bay leaf
- 3 garlic cloves, sliced
- 45g (1½oz) fresh root ginger, peeled
- 200ml (7fl oz) white wine
- 2–3 jalapeños, finely sliced
- 25g (1oz) coriander, leaves picked
- sea salt flakes

1. Preheat the oven to 200°C (400°F), Gas Mark 6. Halve the squash, scoop out the seeds and remove the stalk. Rub with 2 tablespoons of the oil, place on a baking tray and roast for 25–35 minutes until soft and caramelized.

2. Cook the rice in salted water until just tender. Drain and set aside until ready to use.

3. Meanwhile, in a medium pan heat the remaining oil over a medium heat and add the onions with a pinch of salt. Cook for 5 minutes, then add the bay leaf, garlic and ginger. Cook for a further 10 minutes until completely soft. Add the wine and allow the alcohol to cook off for a minute. Add 500ml (18fl oz) of water to the pan and bring to a simmer.

4. When the squash is soft, add it to the onions with a pinch of salt. If the skin is really tough scrape out the flesh and omit the skin. Either in a blender or with a stick blender, blend until smooth. Let down with a little water if the mix is too thick. When ready to serve, add the rice and check the seasoning. Serve with the jalapeños and coriander to top. Can be served with pickled chillies from page 90.

MUSHROOMS & ONION FAMILY

MUSHROOMS are one of the quickest ways to bring a meal together, providing lovely texture and soaking up so much flavour. I try to buy and use the firmest mushrooms I can find. Using them as soon as possible means they cook a lot better and the flavour is much brighter. If you do have some threatening to hang around too long, try pickling them using one of the recipes in the book – a great way to preserve them to enjoy later.

Lemon *MUSHROOMS*

This dish definitely has a stroganoff feel about it, but it is wonderfully bright and zingy from all the lemon and sings with freshness. Serve it with any grains that you like. The nuttier whole grains are a pleasant foil. I tend to just use water to let the sauce down as it gives it a clear profile. Although do try cider, as it adds an extra layer of flavour. I like to make this quite saucy to allow the sauce to really mix with the grains and coat everything. SERVES 4

- 3 tablespoons olive oil
- 2 onions, roughly sliced
- 2 celery sticks, sliced
- 3 fat garlic cloves, sliced
- 2 bay leaves
- 750g (1lb 10oz) mushrooms, a mix is good, button, chestnut, oyster, wild all work well
- 200g (7oz) crème fraîche
- 200ml (7fl oz) water or cider
- zest and juice of 2 lemons (you may want the zest of another one)
- 25g (1oz) parsley, finely chopped
- sea salt flakes and black pepper
- cooked barley, spelt, oat groats or rice, to serve

1. Heat a large frying pan or wide casserole over a medium heat. Add the oil followed by the onions and celery. Cook for 10–12 minutes until soft and just starting to colour. Add the garlic and bay leaves.

2. Meanwhile, thickly slice or quarter your mushrooms if they are large. I like to leave small to medium-sized mushrooms whole so they have a presence in the finished dish. Add them to the pan and cook for 4–6 minutes, stirring occasionally.

3. Add the crème fraîche and water or cider. Bring to a simmer and bubble for 2–3 minutes. Turn off the heat and add half the lemon juice and zest. Taste, add salt and pepper, as well as more lemon juice and zest according to your taste. Stir through the parsley and serve with grains.

MUSHROOM ketchup

As you may know by now, I am partial to a condiment. I love that little finishing touch it can bring to a meal, ploughman's lunch plate or a sandwich, cheese on toast or baked potatoes. Basically, any excuse to get the extra quick hit of flavour from a chutney or sauce is always welcome in my opinion. So, for this book I set about writing a mushroom ketchup recipe. Something I have been meaning to do for a long time but never got around to. I wanted something that could be dolloped and spread. Something that had flavours that would work equally well for any meal. A tiny tickle of heat from the chilli. A hint of something from the allspice. The tamari adds a wonderfully rich umami base note. I like to reuse empty squeezy bottles for serving from. Divide the sauce between small jars to keep the ketchup fresher in smaller batches. MAKES 1.5 LITRES (2 ⅔ PINTS)

- 1 ancho chilli, but experiment with others
- 3 tablespoons olive oil
- 1 celery stick, roughly sliced
- 1 onion, roughly diced
- 3 garlic cloves, sliced
- 900g (2lb) mushrooms, portobello gives darker colour, either fairly finely chopped by hand or blitzed in a food processor
- 2 teaspoons ground allspice
- 60ml (2¼fl oz) cider vinegar
- 25g (1oz) dark muscovado sugar or black treacle
- 125ml (4½fl oz) tamari
- sea salt flakes

1. In a large pan set over a medium heat, start by toasting the ancho chilli. A minute or two on each side should be enough. When it is aromatic, remove and place in a jug with 500ml (18fl oz) of boiling water to infuse.

2. Add the oil to the same pan, followed by the celery, onion and garlic. Cook gently for 12–15 minutes until everything is soft. Add the mushrooms and continue to cook, stirring regularly, for another 20–25 minutes. Once the mushrooms have lost most of their moisture, add the mixture to a blender with the rest of the ingredients, including the ancho chilli and soaking water, reserving half of the tamari. Blend until very smooth. Taste and add more tamari if you think it needs it and a pinch of salt. Keep in mind that it wants to be pretty punchy as it is a condiment. I use all of the tamari.

3. I then pour the ketchup into small sterilized jars and store them in the fridge. Although there should be enough residual heat to form a vacuum and keep them shelf stable. They keep well for a few months, the flavours will continue to marry and develop.

MUSHROOM
vol-au-vents

The inspiration for this dish was garlic snails. Memories of my parents eating them in France on holidays when I was a small child. I thought it would be fun to make a tongue-in-cheek homage to those days and the garlicky snails. The velvety spinach sauce element felt like a good addition to bring everything together. Using shiitake mushrooms changes the texture up a bit. They are rather silky as well when cooked. Oyster mushrooms would be great too. We had this recently for dinner with mashed potatoes. It took on more of a London East End feel, reminding us of pie and mash shops. I can highly recommend serving it this way. The sauce is just enough to coat everything. I bake potatoes in the oven until soft all the way through, then scoop out the flesh and pass through a ricer. Mix in some butter and salt and you are done. The mash doesn't want to be too fluid as the pastry is already rich and the sauce is well set for bringing everything together. MAKES 4

- 1 x 325g (11½oz) sheet of puff pastry
- 1 egg, beaten with 1 tablespoon milk
- 4 tablespoons olive oil
- 6 fat garlic cloves, sliced (or more if you like)
- 400g (14oz) spinach
- 40g (1½oz) parsley
- juice of 1 lemon (about 30ml/1fl oz)
- 450g (1lb) button mushrooms, or other types work well
- sea salt flakes and black pepper

1. Preheat the oven to 180°C (350°F), Gas Mark 4. Lay out your sheet of puff pastry and cut it in half along its length. Brush one side with egg wash and place the other half on top to neatly line up. Cut this into four equal sections. Brush each of these with egg wash. Then in each rectangle, cut a smaller rectangle about 1cm (½in) in from the edge, being careful only to cut through the top layer of pastry. These will be your lids.

2. Place the rectangles on a lined baking sheet and bake for 30–40 minutes until well risen and golden. Rotate the tray 180 degrees two-thirds of the way through cooking. Remove from the oven and carefully run a small knife in and under each smaller cut-out rectangle. Carefully lift them free to form little lids.

3. Meanwhile, in a medium saucepan heat 2 tablespoons of the oil over a medium–low heat. Add the garlic and cook for 2–3 minutes until soft. Just before it starts to colour, start adding the spinach, a handful at a time. Mix well to wilt and follow with more spinach until it is all in. Add the parsley, cook for a further minute, then decant everything into a blender. Add the lemon juice and blend until very smooth. Add salt and pepper. If the mix doesn't get moving enough, keep adding splashes of boiling water to get it blending.

4. Heat the remaining 2 tablespoons of oil in the pan and add the mushrooms with a pinch of salt. Cook for 3–5 minutes until they are soft and taking on a bit of colour. Add the spinach sauce and mix to combine. If it is a little thick, add a splash of boiling water. Taste for seasoning and then spoon into your pastry cases and place the lids on top. Serve while still hot.

MUSHROOM burgers

The best vegetarian burger is a grilled mushroom in my opinion. Rather than trying to imitate meat counterparts, just make a really tasty mushroom sandwich. Juicy and charred, it is perfect. Load it up however you like – I like a slice of tomato as the sweet acidity is very welcome. The slaw means you can build in other flavours and textures but in an easy-to-assemble sandwich way. Use more or less of any of the elements to tweak it to your tastes. I use yogurt as it keeps it fresh and I like the sour note it gives. You could make it without or sub in mayonnaise if you like. It is worth making your own plant-based mayonnaise from the recipe on page 12. Then while you are at it, you may as well knock up some homemade fennel and tomato ketchup from page 110. SERVES 6

- 6 portobello mushrooms or 500g (1lb 2oz) smaller mushrooms
- 4 tablespoons oil, sunflower works well
- 250g (9oz) red or white cabbage, or a mix, finely shredded
- 1 fennel bulb, tough stalks removed, finely shredded
- 4 spring onions, finely sliced
- 10g (¼oz) chives, finely chopped
- 100g (3½oz) natural yogurt
- 6 buns, brioche are good, but crusty rolls work for a heartier option, sliced in half
- sea salt flakes and black pepper

1. Heat a griddle pan, cast-iron or heavy-based frying pan over a medium heat. On a tray, coat the mushrooms in the oil and a pinch of salt. If using smaller mushrooms, only use half the oil and add the oil to the pan directly.

2. Add the mushrooms to the pan top-side down and cook for 3 minutes. Then turn them and cook for a further 3 minutes. Turn over once more to cook for a final minute or so, then season with a sprinkle of salt. The juices will begin to collect in the cap of the mushrooms – be careful to try and keep this golden liquor as it will add to their overall juiciness.

3. Add the cabbage, fennel, spring onion and chives to a mixing bowl with a good pinch of salt and black pepper and mix well. Mix in the yogurt and taste and add more seasoning if needed.

4. Remove the mushrooms once they are easily pierced with a knife. Add your buns cut-side down to toast, flip them to lightly toast the tops and remove from the pan.

5. Spread mayonnaise or any sauce of your choosing on the bottom half of each bun. Add a mushroom. Dress with any juices that have collected. Spoon the slaw into the mushrooms caps. Finish with the bun lid. You will need napkins.

ONIONS are probably my favourite vegetable. I could have a meal comprised just of onions. I love them in any variation – raw to finish dishes, pickled or fully cooked to add a lovely baseline sweetness. Any shape or form is always welcome. I love basing meals around any member of the onion family. Always such a reliable starting point, they are also stars in their own right.

Confit *GARLIC*

By all means reduce the amount of garlic if you are in a rush, but I love having a stockpile at hand in the fridge. I turn it into an activity with my three year old, as he likes organizing the cloves into different pots and the papery garlic skins into a compost bowl. The oil is good on just about anything. The same goes for the succulent sticky garlic cloves. Think sandwiches, salads, crushed and spread on toast, starting off sauces or stews. Anywhere they show up they **improve the situation.** MAKES 1/2 LITRE (1 PINT) JAR

- 3 bay leaves
- 2 big sprigs of rosemary
- 6 heads of garlic, cloves separated and peeled
- 250ml (8½fl oz) extra-virgin olive oil
- sea salt flakes

1. In a medium saucepan, combine the ingredients over a medium-low heat. Gently poach the garlic cloves in the oil until they are golden brown and the bubbling has mostly stopped. Depending on your hob, this will take anywhere from 10-20 minutes. Just keep a good eye on them. Once they start to colour, they will go fairly quickly. Add a good pinch of salt and stir to combine.

2. Keep these submerged in the oil in an airtight container in the fridge for a month or so. Then use straight from the fridge to start off sauces or in salads. Crushed on toast with some soft goat's cheese is particularly good.

Confit *GARLIC* Caesar salad

I've always felt a bit left out of the Caesar salad party, so I wanted to create a version that isn't lacking and holds its own on the circuit. It is really easy to bring together, especially if you have prepped the garlic ahead and have it conveniently waiting in the fridge. I really like Spenwood cheese for this. It is a hard sheep's cheese which uses vegetarian rennet. Equally anything similar that you like would work well. SERVES 4 AS A SIDE

- 200g (7oz) bread, cut in 2–3cm (¾–1¼in) cubes
- 50ml (1¾fl oz) extra-virgin olive oil
- 1 heaped tablespoon Dijon mustard
- 2 egg yolks
- 30ml (1fl oz) lemon juice (about ½ lemon)
- couple of dashes of vegetarian Worcestershire sauce
- 2 tablespoons garlic oil
- 8 fat confit garlic cloves (see page 64)
- 100–150g (3½–5½oz) Spenwood or other hard cheese, grated
- 2 heads of romaine lettuce, roots trimmed and leaves separated
- sea salt flakes and black pepper

1. Preheat the oven to 200°C (400°F), Gas Mark 6. In a mixing bowl, toss the bread cubes with the oil. Add to a preheated oven tray and toast in the oven for 10 minutes. Give the tray a shake and turn the croutons over. Return to the oven for a further 5–10 minutes until golden and crisp.

2. In the mixing bowl, add the mustard, egg yolks, lemon juice and Worcestershire sauce. Whisk together with the garlic oil. Add a good pinch of salt and a few good grinds of black pepper. Add the garlic cloves and crush them to a rough paste with a fork. Mix everything together with 75–100g (2½–3½oz) of the cheese, to your taste.

3. When ready to serve, add the lettuce and slightly cooled croutons and toss well to coat in the dressing. Serve with the remaining cheese on top.

ONION tart

I love this as an intro to dinner parties while everyone is standing around catching up. I cut the tart into smaller sections for more of a canapé feel. Equally it works well for picnics or packed lunches and as something to look forward to on a brisk walk. The onion mixture can be made ahead of time and kept in the fridge until you are ready to go. SERVES 8 AS A STARTER WITH A SALAD OR MORE AS A CANAPÉ

- 1kg (2lb 4oz) onions
- 4 tablespoons olive oil
- 2 sprigs of thyme, leaves picked
- 1 x 325g (11½oz) sheet of puff pastry
- 2 tablespoons Dijon mustard
- 100g (3½oz) black olives, the really dark inky kind, pitted
- 1 egg, beaten with 1 tablespoon milk
- sea salt flakes and black pepper

1. Cut the onions in half from the tip to the root. Then slice them fairly thinly in the same manner, tip to root.

2. In a large saucepan, heat the oil over a medium heat. Add the onion and a good pinch of salt. Cook the onions for 30–40 minutes, stirring occasionally, until collapsed and caramelized. If they need longer, do keep steadily going, they can't really be rushed. As the finish line approaches, add the thyme. Check the seasoning and add salt and pepper accordingly. Set aside and allow to cool a little.

3. Preheat the oven to 200°C (400°F), Gas Mark 6.

4. Roll out the sheet of pastry onto a lined baking sheet. Score a rectangle 1cm (½in) in from the edge all the way around to help form the edge to the tart. Spread the mustard inside this rectangle. Then top with the onions spread evenly, ensuring they stay within the inner rectangle. Dot over the olives.

5. Brush the edge with egg wash and bake for 25 minutes, then rotate 180 degrees and continue to cook for a further 10–15 minutes until the ends are puffy and golden and the centre is bubbling.

6. Remove from the oven and either allow to cool a little on a rack or cut up straight away and serve.

Burrata with caramelized *SHALLOTS* & pine nuts

Hot onions, cool cheese. Sweet and sticky. Yep, this dish has all the good things happening. I created this when we had these ingredients left from the supplies that I'd taken with us on holiday. As well as being very pleased that I managed use up all the food pretty much exactly, this happened to be a great hit as a canapé-meets-pre-dinner nibble – little grilled slices of baguette for everyone to scoop and smoosh the cheese with toppings onto. This is great as guests are arriving when everyone is hanging around the kitchen hungry. Put this down and let them sort themselves out while you get on. SERVES 6 OR SO AS A CANAPÉ

- 4 tablespoons extra-virgin olive oil, plus extra to serve
- 4 banana shallots, cut into quarters lengthways
- 400g (14oz) shallots, quartered along their lengths
- 40g (1½oz) pine nuts or almonds also work well
- 300–400g (10½–14oz) burrata or fresh mozzarella
- sea salt flakes and black pepper
- crusty bread or baguette cut into rounds, brushed with oil and grilled, to serve

1. In a medium saucepan over a medium heat, add the oil followed by the shallots and a pinch of salt. Cook gently, stirring occasionally, for 12–15 minutes.

2. When the shallots are light golden and beginning to caramelize, add the pine nuts. Cook, stirring fairly often, so the pine nuts don't catch, for another 5–7 minutes until they are also golden in colour.

3. Tear open your cheese and place it on a plate. Spoon over the shallot mixture. Add an extra drizzle of oil if you think it needs it and a couple of grinds of black pepper and a sprinkle of salt. Serve with crusty bread or grilled baguette toasts.

ONION rings
& yogurt herb ranch

On our honeymoon we got taken up into the hills outside of Santa Barbara to listen to live music at the Cold Spring Tavern. Such a special place, with excellent music. I also vividly remember the onion rings. I was already a big fan of deep-fried crispy onions in any form and these onion rings were not messing around. Really big rings, well coated and stacked high. The paprika adds a little note to the final flavour but also makes the onion rings a wonderful golden colour once cooked. I like to add in a bunch of spring onions, well washed, as the roots are edible and go wonderfully crunchy when cooked this way. Banana shallots, peeled and halved or quartered lengthways, are also great and become almost creamy in texture. Try whatever onions you like. I made the ranch yogurt to add a bit of freshness and restrain some of the fattiness. Swap in buttermilk and more mayonnaise if you are feeling decadent. MAKES A SHARING PLATE

- 3 large onions
- 50g (1¾oz) cornflour
- 1.5-2 litres (2 ⅔-3½ pints) sunflower oil
- 300g (10½oz) plain flour
- 300ml (10½fl oz) beer
- 3 tablespoons paprika
- 1 tablespoon baking powder

FOR THE RANCH YOGURT
- 300g (10½oz) natural yogurt
- 3 tablespoons mayonnaise (see page 12 for homemade plant-based version)
- 25g (1oz) dill, finely chopped
- 25g (1oz) chives, finely chopped
- 1 teaspoon garlic powder
- 1 teaspoon onion powder
- sea salt flakes and black pepper

1. Mix all the ranch yogurt ingredients together with a few grinds of black pepper and a pinch of salt. Taste and add more salt if it needs it. Cover and keep in the fridge until you need it.

2. Slice the onions into thirds or quarters across their equators. You are looking for substantial chunky rings. Separate into individual rings on a tray or baking sheet. Sprinkle over the cornflour and toss to coat as much of the onions as possible.

3. In a large pan with high sides, add enough oil to go about 5-6cm (2-2½in) high. Heat the oil to 190°C (375°F). Set a wire rack on a baking tray to drain the on rings on.

4. Mix the flour, beer, paprika and baking powder together with a pinch of salt. The batter should be fairly thick and clinging but still mostly fall away when the onions are lifted out. Drop a few onions rings into the batter at a time. Then carefully add them to the oil. Don't overcrowd the pan or they will stick together and reduce the temperature of the oil. Flip them halfway to cook the top side. As a general rule 2 minutes each side for the larger ones should be enough.

5. Once golden and crisp, remove from the oil with a slotted spoon and place on the wire rack. Sprinkle with salt. Repeat until all the onion rings are done. Serve with the ranch yogurt alongside.

I'm partial to cooking **LEEKS** just long enough so they keep their fresh flavour. I love the wonderful bright green the tops go when they meet the heat of cooking. A trick I learned a while ago to clean them is to trim any really rough bits then, a centimetre or two (about an inch) in from the root, cutting all the way through down the centre and running the knife out past the green tips. Then you can fan out the sections to clean them thoroughly if they are particularly dirty.

Steamed *LEEKS* with Georgian walnut sauce

This sauce is addictive. I like having a pot of it in the fridge to add to lunch plates or sandwiches. I was first introduced to it when photographing in Georgia. Traditionally it is made thicker and rolled up in strips of fried aubergine, which is well worth your while making – you won't regret it. I wanted to make a quick and lighter option here. The leeks add a freshness and are available most of the year, so this is a good recipe to have in your back pocket. A few capers scattered over at the end also adds another note to the dish.

SERVES 4 AS A SIDE OR STARTER

- 250g (9oz) walnut halves
- 6 leeks, trimmed, cleaned and cut into 3–4cm (1¼–1½ in) sections on the diagonal
- 2 garlic cloves
- 100ml (3½fl oz) neutral flavoured sunflower oil, or a low flavour olive oil works as well
- 10g (¼oz) parsley, leaves picked
- sea salt flakes and black pepper
- extra-virgin olive oil, for drizzling

1. Pour boiling water over the walnuts and allow to sit for 20 minutes.

2. Steam the leeks for 10–15 minutes until soft in the centre and cooked through. I like to place the leeks onto a plate that will fit in the steamer, or multiple plates in a stacking steamer. Equally, blanch them in salted boiling water.

3. Drain the walnuts and add them to a blender along with the garlic and oil and blitz. Alternatively, add to a tall container and blitz with a hand blender. Add 250ml (9fl oz) of water and a good pinch of salt and blend until very smooth. Taste and add more salt if needed. Keep in the fridge until needed. The sauce will thicken in the fridge. It will keep well for a few days happily.

4. When ready to serve, spread the sauce onto plates or a platter. Top with the leeks and scatter over the parsley leaves. A drizzle of oil, a few twists of black pepper and you are done.

Chunky *VEG* broth & chive biscuits

I first came across American biscuits when working in Charleston, South Carolina. They are similar to English scones, but something very different at the same time. These are seriously flaky. Cutting and stacking the dough really helps build those layers. Chives are my favourite, but you can also use dill or the shredded green tops of spring onions. In the broth, oyster mushrooms also work really well if you have them, as they add a little something extra texture wise.

SERVES 6/MAKES 12 BISCUITS

- 2 tablespoons olive oil, others work fine also
- 2–3 carrots (about 200g/7oz), tops removed and sliced
- 2 red onions, cut into eighths
- 4 leeks (about 800g/1lb 12oz), trimmed, cleaned, white part finely sliced, greens shredded
- 500g (1lb 2oz) button mushrooms, finely sliced
- 1 litre (1¾ pints) vegetable stock
- sea salt flakes and black pepper

FOR THE BISCUITS

- 400g (14oz) self-raising flour, plus extra for dusting
- 10g (¼oz) salt
- 200g (7oz) cold unsalted butter, cut into cubes, plus 25g (1oz) butter, melted
- 50g (1¾oz) chives, finely chopped
- 225ml (8fl oz) buttermilk, kefir, soured cream or natural yogurt
- 1 tablespoon vinegar, any variety works fine

1. You can make the biscuits by hand but a food processor is less hassle. Combine the flour, salt and cubed butter in the food processor. Pulse until the mixture resembles sand. Or if making by hand, rub the butter into the flour mixture as swiftly as possible.

2. Tip into a mixing bowl. Add the chives, buttermilk and the vinegar. Mix to bring together.

3. Tip out onto a well-floured work surface. Gently roll out the dough until about 35 x 25cm (14 x 10in). To help create flaky layers in the scones, cut the dough into quarters and stack them on top of each other. Then gently push down and re-roll the dough until it is 3cm (1¼in) thick and roughly 30 x 15cm (12 x 6in). Use more flour to help sticking if needed.

4. Cut the dough into 12 pieces and place on baking trays lined with greaseproof paper, spaced well apart. If you have space in the freezer, place the trays in for 20–30 minutes to firm up. The fridge also works for the same amount of time. Preheat the oven to 220°C (425°F), Gas Mark 7.

5. Brush each biscuit with melted butter, then bake in the oven for 10 minutes. Remove the trays carefully, rotate 180 degrees and return to the oven, swapping each tray onto the shelf that it wasn't on before. Cook for a further 8–12 minutes until golden. Remove and allow to cool on a wire rack. They need to finish cooking inside for 5 minutes but are good to go when you can handle them.

6. Meanwhile, heat the oil in a good-sized pan. Add the carrots and onion with a good pinch of salt and cook for 6–8 minutes until beginning to soften. Add the leeks and mushrooms. Stir well to incorporate and cook for a further 3–5 minutes. Add the stock. Bring to a simmer for 10 minutes. Check the seasoning, add black pepper at this stage as well and serve the broth with biscuits alongside.

AUBERGINES PEPPERS & CHILLIES

Just a sponge for flavours really, held together by its skin, I can never quite put my finger on why I love **AUBERGINES** so much. There is something extremely special about a just-cooked section of aubergine – glistening skin with the yielding fluffiness of its flesh transitioning to soothing silkiness.

AUBERGINE agrodulce

A lovely balance between sharp and sweet, this dish can be made ahead and improves while waiting. It is a good one to make if you have lots of aubergines that need cooking as it happily sits in the fridge and can elevate a lunch plate or sandwich. SERVES 4 AS A STARTER OR ANTIPASTI

- 3 aubergines, cut into 2cm (¾in) thick slices lengthways
- 1 red onion, diced
- 5–6 tablespoons extra-virgin olive oil
- 2 chillies, mix of colours is good, finely diced and deseeded if you like
- 30g (1oz) walnut halves, broken up
- 2 tablespoons capers
- 2 tablespoons raisins, plumped up in hot water for 10 minutes
- 50ml (2fl oz) honey, sugar or agave syrup
- 5 tablespoons red wine vinegar
- 15g (½oz) parsley, roughly chopped
- 25g (1oz) mint, leaves picked and roughly chopped
- sea salt flakes

1. Heat a griddle pan over a medium-high heat. On a baking tray, coat the aubergine slices with 2–3 tablespoons of the oil and griddle for 2–3 minutes each side until tender. You can also fry the aubergine slices but you will need a bit more oil. Alternatively, roast the slices on a lined baking tray dressed with oil in the oven for 15–20 minutes at 180°C (350°F), Gas Mark 4.

2. Set aside while you make the dressing – I stack them up on top of one another back on the baking tray, to help them carry on gently cooking.

3. Fry the onion in 3 tablespoons of oil with a pinch of salt for 7–10 minutes until soft and starting to colour. Add the chillies and walnuts and toast for a further 2 minutes. Follow with the capers, raisins, honey, vinegar and parsley. Stir well to melt the honey.

4. Check the seasoning and spoon over the aubergine. Finish with the mint leaves.

AUBERGINE & squash coconut curry with herb & pea salad

This is often on rotation at ours and gets regularly requested by the kids. You can make it as spicy or not as you please. If making for children, or keeping those not so chilli tolerant in mind, then just omit them and serve sliced chillies or the pickled ones from page 90 alongside. I first made this as a picnic-friendly dish and people helped themselves to the different elements. Originally I made this with the roasted and grilled bits, including chicken thighs, then the sauce separate, rice in a container and the salad in another, plus limes to squeeze over. Essentially, what I am saying is that you can use the sauce and salad parts interchangeably to suit what is in season or what people fancy. SERVES 6

- 3 aubergines, each cut into sixths
- 8 tablespoons neutral oil, I use sunflower
- 600g (1lb 5oz) squash, cut into 3cm (1¼in) wide sections
- 50g (1¾oz) chillies, deseeded if you like
- 65g (2¼oz) fresh root ginger, washed and any tough bits and soil removed
- 1 head of garlic, cloves separated and peeled
- 5 shallots or 3 small onions, halved
- 2 x 400ml (14fl oz) cans full-fat coconut milk
- 200g (7oz) frozen peas (petit pois are the sweetest), defrosted
- 2 spring onions, finely sliced
- couple of handfuls of mixed soft herbs, such as dill, coriander, basil, lemon basil, purple basil
- sea salt flakes

TO SERVE
- cooked rice or other grains
- 3-4 limes, cut into wedges

1. Preheat the oven to 220°C (425°F), Gas Mark 7. On one oven tray, combine the aubergine chunks with 3 tablespoons of the oil and spread out evenly. On another tray, do the same with the squash and another 2 tablespoons of oil. Roast in the oven for 20-30 minutes, then turn the veg over and return to the oven for a further 10-15 minutes until soft, golden and caramelized at the edges. Remove from the oven.

2. Meanwhile, in a food processor, combine the remaining 3 tablespoons of oil with the chillies, ginger, garlic, shallots and a good pinch of salt. Blend to a paste.

3. Heat a large pan or wok over a medium-high heat and add the paste. Fry for 3-5 minutes, stirring often, until aromatic and beginning to colour. Add the coconut milk and bring to a simmer. Allow to bubble for 10-15 minutes until thickened slightly.

4. Add the aubergines and squash. Being careful not to break them up too much when stirring them in. Allow this to gently bubble for 5 minutes to marry the flavours of the sauce with the veg.

5. Combine the peas with the spring onions and herbs. Serve the curry spooned over rice or a grain of your choosing, with the herb and pea salad and a pile of lime wedges alongside.

RIGATONI ALLA NORMA

I make this a lot as a step up from a simple tomato sauce pasta. I feel myself craving it toward the end of summer while aubergines are still in season. For this reason, I think of it as the beginning of the transition into more autumnal dishes. I have fond memories of ordering this in Sicily, sometimes just ordering the sauce as an antipasti when the weather was too hot for pasta, similar to how I'd serve caponata. So, by all means use it as a sauce to go other places than pasta. I like this to be heavy on the aubergine and to keep them in fairly large chunks so they have a good presence in the final dish. SERVES 6

- 1kg (2lb 4oz) aubergines, cut into 4–5cm (1½–2in) cubes
- 100–150ml (3½ –5½fl oz) extra-virgin olive oil, plus extra for drizzling
- 5 garlic cloves, sliced
- 1 tablespoon chilli flakes
- 2 x 400g (14oz) cans plum tomatoes
- 400–500g (14–17½oz) rigatoni or other chunky pasta
- 2 tablespoons red wine vinegar
- 30g (1oz) basil, leaves picked
- sea salt flakes
- grated ricotta salata or goat Cheddar, to serve

1. Set a large sauté or frying pan over a medium heat. Working in two batches, use 50ml (1¾fl oz) of oil per batch to fry the aubergines with a pinch of salt. You can do this in smaller batches if your pan isn't large enough to accommodate that much aubergine at once. It can be snug but doesn't want to be overcrowded. If they are sticking too much, use more oil. Some aubergines soak up more oil than others. Turn the aubergine so it is golden on each side and soft. This should take about 6–8 minutes for each batch. Remove to a mixing bowl or plate and repeat with the next batch.

2. Once the aubergine is cooked, add a further 2 tablespoons of oil and fry the garlic for a minute. Add the chilli flakes, then the tomatoes. I like to use a masher to crush them up a bit. Add a full can's worth of water to the pan with a good pinch of salt. Bubble away for 15–20 minutes until thickened and glossy.

3. Cook your pasta in well-salted water until al dente. Reserve a cup of pasta water in case you need it.

4. Add the aubergine to the tomato sauce with the vinegar. Check the seasoning and add more salt if it needs it. Add the drained pasta and any pasta water you need to get a fluid sauciness. Stir through most of the basil leaves. Spoon onto plates or a serving dish and finish with the remaining basil leaves and some cheese, with more at the table to add. As always, a drizzle of olive oil to finish is very welcome.

Such a welcome burst of freshness, **PEPPERS** always make me think of peak summer and the ease of pulling together simple salads with them. Equally they can take heat really well, whether on the barbecue or roasting in the oven. If you have any to hand it is always a good idea to stick some in the oven if something else is cooking. Peel and keep the sweet, concentrated flesh to add into other dishes or sauces.

PEPPERS, green beans, oat groats & stracciatella

Bright and fresh while still having a good amount of substance to it, this assembly can happily evolve with other ingredients being added. It also works with a dollop of yogurt instead of the stracciatella, or fresh mozzarella or burrata if easier to find. Equally some crumbled feta would do the trick. You get the idea. Play around with what you have and like. SERVES 4

- 4 peppers, the same or a mix of colours
- 300g (10½oz) green beans, stalks removed
- 300g (10½oz) oat groats or spelt or pearl barley, cooked until tender in lightly salted water
- 2–4 tablespoons best olive oil, plus extra for drizzling
- 15g (½oz) mint, leaves picked, finely chopped
- juice of 1–2 lemons
- 300–400g (10½–14oz) stracciatella
- sea salt flakes and black pepper

1. Preheat the oven to 220°C (425°F), Gas Mark 7. Line a baking sheet with parchment paper.

2. Add the peppers to the prepared baking sheet and roast for 20–30 minutes until collapsed and the flesh is soft.

3. Blanch the beans in salted boiling water for 3–5 minutes until they have just a little resistance. Drain and chill in ice water for 5 minutes. Drain once again and chop along their lengths into little rounds. Add to a large mixing bowl with the oat groats, olive oil, mint, half the lemon juice and a few grinds of black pepper.

4. Once the peppers are cool enough to handle, peel off their skins and compost. Pull apart and scrape out as much of the seeds and stalks as you can. A few rogue ones aren't an issue. Cut the pepper flesh into strips and then go back down them with a knife to dice. Add to the mixing bowl with any juices from their bowl.

5. Stir everything to combine. Taste and add more salt, lemon juice or olive oil as you see fit. Spoon onto a serving dish or individual plates and divide the stracciatella between them. Finish with a final drizzle of oil.

GREEN PEPPERS,
potatoes & eggs

This is a Spanish-inspired dish, which is an amalgamation of a few different experiences at meals. Regardless, potatoes, eggs and peppers are great together, all tied up with a good splash of sherry vinegar. This is lovely as a weekend breakfast offering, or a barbecue dish cooked while camping. The potatoes may even benefit from a slight crush to help them absorb the juices. SERVES 4

- 5 green peppers, the long Turkish varieties are also good
- 5 tablespoons extra-virgin olive oil
- 800g (1lb 12oz) new potatoes
- 2 tablespoons sherry vinegar
- 4 eggs
- 1 teaspoon smoked paprika, spicy is good, but as you prefer
- sea salt flakes

1. Preheat the oven to 200°C (400°F), Gas Mark 6. Place the peppers on a tray and roast for 15–20 minutes until collapsing. Turn them halfway through cooking. Once the peppers are done, remove them from the oven, place in a bowl and cover with a plate to steam and cool for 5 minutes.

2. In a pan, cover the potatoes with salted water and bring to a gentle simmer. Cook for 10–15 minutes until falling off a knife when pierced.

3. While the potatoes are cooking, peel and deseed the peppers. Keep any liquid that has been released from them. Add the peeled flesh to the pepper juices along with the sherry vinegar and a good pinch of salt. Add the cooked potatoes and mix to combine. Allow to sit while you cook the eggs.

4. Heat about 5 tablespoons of oil in a frying pan until hot. Add the eggs one at a time and cook all four over a medium-high heat for 2–3 minutes until the bottoms are crispy but the tops are also cooked through. I like to either tilt the pan and spoon hot oil over the tops of the eggs to cook them or place a lid over the pan.

5. Either plate individually, or on a platter or serving plate. Place the potato and pepper mix on first, followed by the eggs. Add a good drizzle of the oil from the pan to finish along with the paprika.

I'm pretty addicted to the heat and bite of **CHILLIES**. The heat of chillies is welcome in any variation – the fresh, pokey burst from a raw chilli, or the deep building, spice of dried flakes or a chilli sauce. The pickled chilli recipe is the most-made recipe from this book in our house. They walk a line between spicy and tempered with a lovely, balancing acid kick. The hot liquor knocks the raw heat back a little and makes them a great addition for any meal.

Pickled *CHILLIES*

We love having these in the fridge to add a little kick to meals. They go with just about anything. Under the cheese when making cheese on toast is a winner, or diced and added to salad dressings or tomato sauces. You can also drain off the liquid and blitz the chillies to a paste to make a sauce. Just keep in a jar in the fridge. I also reuse the pickling liquor – strain out the seeds and debris once the chillies are gone, add a splash of vinegar and a pinch of salt to boost the levels back up, re-boil and use as below. MAKES A 1 LITRE (1¾ PINT) JAR

- 400g (14oz) mixture of your favourite chillies
- 150g (5½oz) onions, preferably small red onions but others work well, peeled
- 2 bay leaves
- 250ml (9fl oz) white wine vinegar, other vinegar also works fine
- 8g (¼oz) sea salt flakes

1. Slice all the chillies, composting the stalks. Cut the onion into as small sections as you like – eighths tends to work for me. Add them to a 1 litre (1¾ pint) heatproof jar with the chillies and bay leaves.

2. In a saucepan, add the vinegar and salt along with 250ml (9fl oz) of water. Heat until boiling.

3. Add the liquid to the jar. Put the lid on and let it sit on the counter until it cools to room temperature. If it needs more salt to your taste, add a pinch at a time and shake the jar to dissolve. Then keep them in the fridge for 3 months plus.

PAPRIKA devilled eggs

These are a kind of turbo-charged devilled egg of 1970s fame. Excellent as a dinner party canapé, or even as a starter with some leaves to make more of an egg salad. Chop through the eggs and mix with the filling to make a fantastic sandwich filler. There is a reason why devilled eggs were so popular. This version is so good I have started using it instead of egg mayonnaise. MAKES 12

- 6 eggs, at room temperature
- 75g (2½oz) mayonnaise (see page 12 for homemade)
- 10g (¼oz) capers, roughly chopped
- ½–1 small banana shallot, finely diced
- juice of ½ lemon (about 30ml/1fl oz)
- 1 heaped teaspoon hot paprika, plus extra for dusting
- 2 cornichons, finely diced
- 10g (¼oz) chives, finely chopped
- sea salt flakes and black pepper
- 1 chilli, thinly sliced, to garnish

1. Place the eggs in a medium saucepan filled with cold water, with a lid on. Heat over a medium heat until at a gentle simmer. As they are heating up, very gently swirl the eggs in the water, moving them in a circular motion around the base of the pan, 2–3 times. This will help to centre the yolks, making life a lot easier and neater when filling them later. Once at a good bubble, turn off the heat and leave the eggs to sit in the water for 4–5 minutes with the lid on.

2. Drain the eggs and return to the pan. Shake it to break the shells. Run under cold water to fill the pan around the eggs, empty the water and refill with cold water. Let sit for a couple of minutes until you can handle the eggs for peeling. Remove the shells and slice each in half across their equators. Cut a thin sliver off each top and bottom so each half will stand up without rolling over. These trimmings can be chopped and added to the filling mixture.

3. In a small mixing bowl, add the egg yolks and the remaining ingredients, except the chilli. Taste and add more shallot, lemon juice, paprika, salt and pepper to your taste.

4. With a teaspoon, carefully divide the yolk mixture between the egg whites. Top with a slice of chilli and a dusting of paprika for old times' sake. Never one to stand in the way of expression, by all means pipe the mixture into the egg whites to go full retro. Just be sure to use a wide nozzle as the mixture is quite chunky.

BIANG BIANG noodles

We love going as a family to Xi'an Biang Biang Noodles in Aldgate East. I wanted to develop a recipe for home as everyone was constantly asking to go to the resaurant. I keep the ingredients in the cupboard as they are good to have on hand, so it is a great meal to pull together quickly. So simple and deeply comforting. The dough can be made ahead and kept in the fridge for rolling out the next day, or the cut noodles freeze extremely well. Lay out on a tray, freeze, then put in a container or freezer bag. Cook direct from the freezer, no need to defrost first. Adjust the spice levels according to your taste. You can start by adding half the quantity of chilli oil and add more until you get to your desired level of intensity. I find this level of spice punchy but not overwhelming. SERVES 4

- 500g (1lb 2oz) plain flour, plus extra for dusting
- 3 tablespoons soy sauce, I use an organic all-purpose one, go with your preference
- 2 tablespoons rice wine vinegar
- 1 garlic clove, finely grated
- 30g (1oz) Korean red pepper chilli flakes
- 10g (¼oz) red chilli flakes
- 40g (1½oz) sesame seeds
- 1 heaped teaspoon ground coriander
- 1 heaped teaspoon cumin seeds, crushed
- 1–2 tablespoons Szechuan peppercorns, crushed
- 5 spring onions, finely sliced
- 250ml (9fl oz) neutral oil, groundnut or sunflower are best
- steamed pak choi or other Chinese greens, to serve
- sea salt flakes

1. If you want to make the dough by hand, start by adding 250ml (9fl oz) of water to the flour in a large mixing bowl. Stir well to combine. Leave for 15 minutes for the flour to hydrate. Then turn out onto a lightly floured surface and knead for 10 minutes until you have a stiff dough. Alternatively, I like to use a stand mixer fitted with the dough hook attachment to make the dough when pushed for time. With the flour in the mixer bowl, start the machine on a low speed. Add 250ml (9fl oz) water in a steady trickle. Turn off and allow to hydrate for 10–15 minutes covered. Then, on a medium–low speed, let the mixer run for 5–10 minutes until the dough is smooth. Shape the dough into a ball and rest for at least 30 minutes with the bowl turned upside down over it.

2. Bring a large pan of well-salted water to a boil. Cut the dough into quarters. Dust with flour if it is sticking. Using a pasta machine, roll out each quarter until the penultimate setting. Alternatively, roll out as thinly as possible using a rolling pin.

3. Using a sharp knife, make cuts down the length of each section of dough to form rough wide noodles – about 2–3cm (¾ –1¼in) is good. But vary the widths and don't worry about straight lines. Dust with a little flour and gently set aside in little piles.

4. Add the all the remaining ingredients, except the oil, to a large mixing bowl. Heat the oil in a small pan until it begins to smoke. Carefully tip over the other ingredients and stir to combine. It will sizzle and become very aromatic.

5. Bring a saucepan of water to the boil. Blanch the pak choi or Chinese greens and remove from the water with a slotted spoon. Bring the water back to the boil, then drop the noodles in carefully. Cook for about 1–2 minutes until tender, but still with some bite. Pull one out and eat it to test. Drain well and add to the chilli oil. Toss well the combine. Check the seasoning and add more soy, salt or vinegar according to you taste. Serve with the pak choi or greens.

TOMATOES & FENNEL

I often consider a plate of **TOMATOES**, a decent sprinkling of sea salt and a heavy hand of good-quality olive oil to be my favourite plate of food. Add a piece of crusty bread to mop everything up with or take it up a notch with some fresh toasted cheese. There isn't much else that can compete. Tomatoes sing of the summer. I don't think it is possible to overeat tomatoes. I mean I've never reached that point, and I've done some trying.

TOMATO paprika lentils, grilled Hispi cabbage

I make a version of these lentils fairly often. The earthiness of the lentils goes so well with the paprika and tomato. I just eat bowls of them, simply topped with yogurt, a few herbs and a drizzle of oil. The cabbage makes them into more of a main offering. If easier, you can roast the cabbage sections in a hot oven until golden in colour and yielding when pierced with a knife. It gets you to a similar place. For a summertime version, shred the cabbage and mix with lemon juice and oil instead. SERVES 4

- 4 tablespoons olive oil
- 2 onions, diced
- 5 garlic cloves, sliced
- 2 heaped teaspoons paprika, or more to taste, I use 1 teaspoon smoked paprika and 1 teaspoon hot
- 300g (10½oz) Puy lentils or other lentils that hold their shape
- 2 x 400g (14oz) cans plum tomatoes
- 1 large head of Hispi cabbage
- sea salt flakes and black pepper
- natural yogurt, to serve

1. In a medium saucepan over a medium-low heat, add 2 tablespoons of the oil, followed by the onions and a good pinch of salt. Cook, stirring occasionally, for 10 minutes. Add the garlic and cook for a further 2-3 minutes.

2. Add the paprika, lentils and tomatoes. Fill the cans with water and add to the pan. Bring to a simmer and cook for 15-20 minutes until the lentils are tender and the sauce is loose but clinging to the lentils. Top up with water if needed. Taste for seasoning and add a few cracks of black pepper.

3. Meanwhile, heat a griddle pan until smoking. Quarter the cabbage through the root into even sections. Rub the remaining 2 tablespoons of oil over the cabbage sections and grill, cut-side down, for 4-6 minutes. Turn each onto the other cut side and repeat the cooking. Finally, turn each section onto their backs and cook until tender. If they need longer, swap between each side for a minute or so each until giving but still with some bite.

4. Portion the lentils between plates and top with a section of the cabbage. Serve with yogurt alongside.

Cheese & *TOMATO* galette

Impressive and worthy of a gathering, but without the faff of lining a tart case. I think of this as a fancied-up cheese, onion and tomato sandwich. Try to get very ripe and juicy tomatoes. The coarsely ground wholemeal flour in the crust brings wonderful texture and flavour. It is worth seeking out if you can find it. Make sure to add enough liquid to bind the pastry dough, which will help with rolling out and transferring to the baking sheet. SERVES 6

- 300g (10½oz) wholemeal flour, I like to use a coarsely ground flour for texture, plus extra for dusting
- 150g (5½oz) unsalted butter
- 1 tablespoon vinegar, your preferred, cider, white or red wine all work well
- 2 tablespoons cold water
- 2 tablespoons olive oil
- 2 onions, finely sliced
- 700g (1lb 9oz) tomatoes, the same variety or a mixture, cut in half across the equator
- 100g (3½oz) your favourite hard cheese, or a mix, such as Cheddar, goat's, Gruyère or Comté, grated
- 1 egg, beaten with 1 tablespoon milk
- sea salt flakes and black pepper

1. First, make the pastry. Put the flour, butter and a pinch of salt in a food processor. Pulse until the mixture resembles fine breadcrumbs. Add the vinegar and cold water, then pulse a few more times to combine. Turn out and gently knead a few times to bring together into one mass. Cover and chill in the fridge for 1 hour. You can reduce this time to 30 minutes if you are in a rush.

2. In a medium saucepan over a medium heat, add the oil followed by the onions. Cook with a pinch of salt for 12–15 minutes until soft and translucent but without much colour. Covering with a lid can help. Set aside to cool a little. Meanwhile, sprinkle a pinch or two of salt into the tomatoes and mix them up.

3. Preheat the oven to 180°C (350°F), Gas Mark 4. Dust baking parchment, which fits the baking sheet, with flour, place the dough in the middle, sprinkle more flour on top and roll out in long strokes going one direction at a time. Avoid rolling back and forth too much. The dough goes outside the baking parchment, which is fine. The diameter of the dough should be roughly 40–45cm (16–17¾in).

4. Drain any juice that has been released from the tomatoes by placing them in a sieve. Spread the pastry evenly with the onions, leaving a 2cm (¾in) border. Add the cheese, then the tomatoes, cut-side up. Starting with the least tidy section, fold that portion of pastry, say 4–6cm (1½–2½in) long, toward the centre. Repeat until you have completed the circumference of the galette. You should have an octagon 28–32cm (11–12in) in diameter that is within the baking parchment. Now, either on the chopping board with the tray at an angle, or with the tray pressed up against the side of the chopping board at the same level, pull the parchment with the galette onto the baking sheet in one swift movement. Brush the pastry with egg wash. Bake for 25 minutes. Rotate the tray 180 degrees and cook for a further 20–30 minutes until the pastry is golden. Remove from the oven, allow to settle for 15 minutes or so, finish with a good grind of black pepper and serve.

Folded cheese & *TOMATO* omelette sandwich

This has become somewhat of a staple in the summer as a breakfast sandwich in our house. I love tomatoes on toast. Fresh and simply sliced with some salt and oil, or grated and seasoned Spanish breakfast-style. Or plum tomatoes from a can heated and laid over buttered toast in the winter months. Proper childhood nostalgia. So, this is a kind of progression from that which the rest of the family enjoys along with me. Fresh, juicy tomatoes bursting with flavour and just enough acid to cut through the cheese and egg. A smattering of spring onion to round everything out. It feels decadent but also nourishingly comforting. The key is the layers of omelette with cheese and spring onion sandwiched between. Spread any condiment you see fit onto the bun lid if you like. SERVES 1

- 1 tablespoon olive oil, plus a splash for the bun
- 1 soft brioche bun, manchet bun, muffin or crusty roll, cut in half
- 1 tomato, at peak ripeness, thinly sliced
- 2 eggs, beaten with a pinch of salt
- 30g (1oz) Cheddar, grated, other hard cheeses work well
- 1 spring onion, finely sliced
- chilli sauce, lime pickle or chutney (optional, to spread on the bun before layering)
- black pepper

1. Heat a 28cm (11in) frying pan over a medium-high heat. Add a tiny splash of oil and place each half of the bun cut-side down. Move them around to collect the oil on the cut side. Toast for 30 seconds or until crisp and golden. Flip over and leave for 20 seconds, then remove to your plate. Arrange the tomato on the bottom half. Reduce the heat to low.

2. Add the remaining oil and swirl around the pan. I use a 25cm (10in) frying pan so the egg can spread out thinly. Follow with the egg and allow to fill out the pan by rotating the pan. Swiftly add the cheese, spring onion and a couple of grinds of black pepper. Give it a brief moment for the cheese to begin to melt and the egg to set. Then fold into the centre from both sides. Then the top into the centre and over again to form a loose square. Remove from the pan and place on top of the tomato. Finish with the top of the bun, spread with your condiment of choice, if you like, and enjoy.

Hand-cut pici with simple *TOMATO* sauce

Really easy to pull together and such a simple nourishing dish. I use this sauce for pizzas as well as anywhere that needs a simple tomato sauce. Play around with how thick you want the pici. Thick noodles are satisfying, but I would start as thin as you can for the first time as they expand a lot when cooking. I blitz my hard cheese in big batches in the blender or food processor. I like it that way for sprinkling as it has more texture than grated. Just keep in an airight container in the fridge. SERVES 4 WELL

- 400g (14oz) 00 flour, plus extra for dusting
- 4 eggs (the mix may need another if a little dry)
- 2 tablespoons olive oil
- good pinch of salt
- 100g (3½oz) Italian-style hard cheese or hard sheep's or cow's cheese of your preference, grated

FOR THE TOMATO SAUCE
- 5 tablespoons extra-virgin olive oil
- 5 garlic cloves, finely sliced
- 100ml (3½fl oz) white wine or cider
- 2 x 400g (14oz) cans plum tomatoes

1. Combine the flour, eggs, oil and salt in a stand mixer fitted with the dough hook and start off on a medium-low speed. Once the ingredients are on their way to forming a dough, increase the speed to medium. I then let the dough knead for about 10 minutes in the machine. If it is a little dry and looking more like breadcrumbs, either add a splash of water or an egg. Equally if it is too wet, add a spoon of flour and mix until a firm consistency.

2. Take the dough from the bowl, place on a chopping board and then invert the bowl over it. Let it rest for 30 minutes.

3. Meanwhile, heat 2 tablespoons of the oil in a medium pan. Add the garlic and cook for a minute. Then add the wine, let it bubble for 30 seconds and follow with the tomatoes. Fill each can with a splash of water and add to the pan. I like to use a potato masher to break up the tomatoes. Cook for 15-20 minutes until reduced slightly and no longer watery.

4. Put a large pan of well-salted water on to boil. Cut the dough into quarters. Lightly dust the work surface with flour and begin rolling each quarter out until it is about 3-5mm (⅛-¼in) thick. Dust the pasta with a little flour, then fold in half and then in half again so you have a long rectangle. Slice along the length in 3-5mm (⅛-¼in) cuts. Then gently shuffle apart the pasta and you'll have thick noodles. Dust with extra flour and set aside. Repeat with the rest of the dough.

5. Once the water is boiling, cook the pasta for 5-10 minutes, depending on thickness. I like to pull a piece out and test it. Once nearly done, add a spoonful of pasta water to the tomato sauce. Drain the pasta well and add to the sauce, reserving a cup of extra pasta water in case you need it.

6. Toss well to combine, adding in the remaining 3 tablespoons of olive oil and half the cheese. Let it down with pasta water if it is too thick. Serve with the remaining cheese alongside.

TOMATO couscous with green bean & parsley salad

Really simple and lovely to make. Use the tomato couscous as a side for other dishes. Adding the green beans on top makes it into more of a complete dish, but it would still go well with other things. Great as a midweek supper that doesn't take too long to bring together when you get in. SERVES 4 AS A LIGHT MEAL

- 3 tablespoons olive oil
- 2 onions, finely diced
- 1 teaspoon ground cumin
- 1 teaspoon ground coriander
- 1 teaspoon fennel seeds, crushed
- 2 x 400g (14oz) cans plum tomatoes
- 25g (1oz) parsley, leaves picked, tender stalks finely chopped
- 250g (8¾oz) couscous
- juice of 1 lemon
- 275ml (10fl oz) boiling water
- 200g (7oz) green beans, stalk ends nipped off
- 60g (2¼oz) black olives, pitted and cut or torn in half
- 1 large banana shallot, finely sliced
- 1-2 tablespoons extra-virgin olive oil, plus extra to serve
- 1-2 tablespoons red wine vinegar or other vinegar you like
- sea salt flakes

1. Heat 2 tablespoons of the oil in a medium-low saucepan over a medium heat. Add the onions with a good pinch of salt. Cook for 12-15 minutes until soft and translucent. Add in the cumin, coriander and fennel seeds, stir for 30 seconds. Add the tomatoes and give them a bit of a crush to break them up a bit. Some chunks are good in the final couscous. Half-fill the cans with water, pour in and let the sauce bubble for 15-20 minutes until thickened slightly. Add the chopped parsley stalks for the final 5 minutes of cooking.

2. In a mixing bowl, add the couscous and remaining 1 tablespoon of oil. Mix really well – I find rubbing between my hands best to get all the couscous grains coated in oil. Equally, stirring well with a fork gets the same result. This will help the couscous not to clump together. Add the lemon juice, a pinch of salt and the boiling water. Give a little stir and then cover. I use a plate or flat baking tray over the bowl. Leave for 15-20 minutes, or longer is fine.

3. Bring a pan of salted water to the boil and blanch the green beans for 3-5 minutes until they just retain some bite. At this point you can either chill them in an ice bath or carry on and serve them warm. If prepping ahead, chilling is a good option.

4. Fork through the couscous and run the grains through your hands to separate them. Add the tomato sauce and stir well to combine. The mixture should be loose, like a well-made risotto. If you add a couple of spoonfuls to a plate and shake it, it should flatten out to the sides. Let it down with some water if too thick.

5. Mix the olives, shallot, parsley leaves, extra-virgin olive oil and vinegar with the beans and portion on top of the couscous on plates. Or do one large platter for the table. A final drizzle of your best oil never hurts.

Possibly my son's favourite vegetable. Whenever it is available, I have **FENNEL** in as he loves just snacking on it. The fresh anise crunch is rather addictive I must admit. Consequently it has found itself into a number of dishes in this book, rightly so. Excellent raw in salads paired with something salty and something acid, but just as good cooked. So versatile and really useful to have on hand.

FENNEL baked with cherry tomatoes & red onion

Really simple to make, this is great as a side or can be made into more of a main paired with a grain. Lovely tossed through couscous to form a salad with some herbs. The tomatoes collapse and form a loose sauce with the oil. Delicious served hot from the oven, or keep it in the fridge and serve at room temperature when you are ready. Mix in cooked pasta for a pasta salad. SERVES 6

1. Preheat the oven to 180°C (350°F), Gas Mark 4. Combine everything in a suitable-sized roasting tray with a good pinch of salt. Mix to coat everything in oil. Roast for 45 minutes–1 hour until the fennel is tender and caramelized.

2. Serve hot from the oven or allow to cool to room temperature.

- 5 fennel bulbs, tough woody stalks removed, quartered
- 500g (1lb 2oz) mixed tomatoes, small cherry ones are best
- 2 red onions, cut into eighths
- 4 tablespoons extra-virgin olive oil
- sea salt flakes

FENNEL
& tomato ketchup

I wanted to make a version of this popular condiment so I could control what was going into it. I find commercial versions can be a bit acrid and smaller-production ones pretty sweet, and both fairly straightforward in flavour. This is where I ended up. I like the balance of these flavours, but please do use it as a platform to experiment with what you like. Chilli is an obvious addition. Keep it in smaller jars so it stays sealed and fresh for longer, or reuse sauce squeezy bottles. This also doubles nicely as a ready-to-go jarred pasta sauce, just let it down with pasta water.

MAKES 1.2 LITRES (2 PINTS)

- 1kg (2lb 4oz) fennel (about 2–4 bulbs depending on their size)
- 1 onion, roughly sliced
- 3 garlic cloves, roughly sliced
- 5 tablespoons olive oil
- 1kg (2lb 4oz) tomatoes
- ½ teaspoon ground cinnamon
- 1 teaspoon ground allspice
- 25g (1oz) sugar or honey
- 75ml (2½fl oz) cider vinegar
- sea salt flakes and black pepper

1. Preheat the oven to 200°C (400°F), Gas Mark 6. Trim the woody stalks from the fennel and roughly slice the bulbs. Add to a large saucepan that will incorporate everything with the onion, garlic and 3 tablespoons of the oil. Cook over a medium heat, stirring often, for 15 minutes.

2. On a roasting tray, combine the remaining 2 tablespoons of oil with the tomatoes and roast for 15 minutes.

3. Add the tomatoes to the pan along with the cinnamon and allspice. Cook, stirring often, for another 15 minutes. If it starts to catch, reduce the heat and keep stirring.

4. Add the mix to a blender with the remaining ingredients, a few good grinds of pepper and a healthy pinch of salt. Blend until very smooth. Taste and add extra spices if you feel they're needed. The mixture wants to be slightly oversalted as it will taste less so once cooled.

5. Add straight into jars or bottles that have been run through the dishwasher or boiled to sterilize them first and attach the lids. The residual heat will form a seal. I store mine in the fridge but they are shelf stable for a number of months. Once opened, store in the fridge for up to 3 weeks.

FENNEL & potato gratin

Decadent and soul warming. This is such a brilliant way to show off fennel. It makes for a lovely main at a dinner party as well. Some watercress or salad leaves on the side are all you need. Well, and some bread to mop up the juices. Try mixing in some blue cheese for a little funk. SERVES 6

- 100g (3½oz) unsalted butter
- 4 onions, sliced
- 2 celery sticks, finely sliced
- 3 sprigs of thyme
- 900g (1lb 14oz) fennel, or 4–5 bulbs, tough woody stalks removed
- 900g (1lb 14oz) potatoes, I favour King Edward, Maris Piper and estima
- 100ml (3½fl oz) white wine or cider
- 200g (7oz) crème fraîche
- 400g (14oz) cheese of your choice, a mixture is good
- 2 garlic cloves, finely chopped or grated
- sea salt flakes and black pepper
- couple of bunches of watercress or bitter leaves, to serve

1. Melt the butter in a large saucepan that will accommodate everything over a medium heat. Add the onions and celery with a good pinch of salt and the thyme. Begin to soften for 12–15 minutes.

2. Preheat the oven to 200°C (400°F), Gas Mark 6. Meanwhile, slice the fennel and potatoes as thinly as possible. The thinner the slices are, the more layers there will be in the finished dish. I like to use a mandolin, but you can also use a knife. Slice each bulb in half, then lay it cut-side down with the root facing toward you and cut across each half. Add the fennel, potato and garlic to the pan. Cook for another 10–15 minutes until wilted.

3. Add the wine or cider and allow to bubble before then adding in the crème fraîche and 300g (10½oz) of the cheese. Turn off the heat and taste for seasoning. Add more salt if needed and a good few grinds of black pepper. Transfer the mix to a baking dish and spread out evenly. Top with the remaining cheese.

4. Bake for 25 minutes, then rotate 180 degrees and continue cooking for 20–30 minutes until golden on top and bubbling. Allow to cool for 10–20 minutes and dig in. Serve with watercress or bitter leaves.

FENNEL & orange salad with black olives

My friend and one-time boss Lori loves this salad. I always think of her when making it. She used to request it from the kitchen at lunchtime, and then get lost in the moment just happy eating this salad. Typically, it would just be fennel and orange, but I've added the olives. Sliced red onion is also a welcome guest to the party. I segment the oranges because I enjoy doing it. If you don't or are in a rush, remove the skin from the oranges with a knife and then cut 5mm (¼in) cross-sections of the orange. These also look great and get you to a similar place. SERVES 4 AS A SIDE

- juice of 1 lemon
- 3 tablespoons extra-virgin olive oil
- 3 oranges, the sweeter the better
- 3 fennel bulbs (about 600g/1lb 5oz)
- 100g (3½oz) Kalamata olives or your favourite black variety
- sea salt flakes

1. Add the lemon juice to a mixing bowl with the oil and a pinch of salt.

2. Top and bottom the oranges so you can see bright juicy flesh. Then sit them on a flat side and carefully and methodically cut down and round each one in sections, removing the peel. You will end up with a naked orange with little white lines running down.

3. Holding the orange over the mixing bowl, put your knife just to the right of one of the white lines and cut gently to the centre. You will feel a slight resistance when you reach it. Then at the next white line, just to the left of it this time, repeat the action. An orange segment should then fall free into the bowl below. Repeat this process until you have gone full circle.

4. Squeeze what is left of the orange into the mixing bowl – this will help form your dressing.

5. Finely slice your fennel, either on a mandolin or with a knife. I like it as thin as possible but chunky also works. Add to the mixing bowl, followed by the olives broken in half and pitted. Mix well to combine and serve.

GREENS

The possibilities are endless. I do find preparing a big pile of **GREEN VEG** for cooking one of the most calming kitchen tasks. Take chard for example: washing, then separating the leaves from the stalks. Trimming the ragged ends. Chopping the leaves and slicing or dicing the stems. All in their little piles. Ready to be cooked at different stages. This paragraph probably says more about me than greens, to be honest!

Grilled *BEANS* with sunflower seed sauce

Great for a barbecue. The sauce and beans can be prepped ahead and then finished over the fire to warm through and char. I use a high-speed blender for the sauce to get a really smooth consistency, but there's no reason why you can't have more texture if you like. You can make the sauce in a pestle and mortar if you are without a blender or want that more rustic feel. SERVES 4

- 500g (1lb 2oz) runner beans, green beans, or a mix
- 200g (7oz) sunflower seeds
- 500ml (18fl oz) water
- lemon juice, to taste (optional)
- 20g (¾oz) parsley, finely chopped
- 3 tablespoons extra-virgin olive oil
- sea salt flakes

1. Trim the tough stalks or fibrous bits from the beans. Using a peeler along the lengths can do this but it can also remove a lot. If the beans are fresh, you can coax the end of the tough cord out with a small knife. Then pull the vein free from the beans and compost. Blanch in salted water for 2–3 minutes. Drain and place in an ice bath to chill until completely cold. Drain well.

2. In a high-speed blender, blitz the sunflower seeds with the water and a good pinch of salt. Add a little squeeze of lemon juice if you like.

3. When ready to serve, toss the beans in 2 tablespoons of oil to coat all over. Either on a hot griddle or barbecue, grill for 1–1½ minutes each side, then add to a mixing bowl with the parsley and a good pinch of salt. Mix to combine.

4. Spread the sunflower paste on a platter or individual plates. Follow with the beans and drizzle over the remaining 1 tablespoon of oil.

SPINACH pie

This is great any time. I could happily eat this every week, but it is especially good for lifting the spirits in the hungry gap when spinach is generally still available. Taking most of its inspiration from spanakopita, it is a dish that the whole family is happy to eat at any time of the year. You can add toasted nuts into the filling as well as using other greens. Equally try without the cheese. Please do just use the recipe as a template. SERVES 6

- 50–75g (1¾–2½oz) unsalted butter, melted
- 270g (9½oz) pack filo, containing 7 pastry sheets
- 50g (1¾oz) sesame seeds

FOR THE FILLING

- 2 tablespoons olive oil
- 4 onions, thickly sliced
- 400g (14oz) feta, crumbled
- zest of 2 lemons
- ⅓–½ nutmeg, grated
- 1 tablespoon dried oregano or mint
- 25g (1oz) dill, chopped
- 1kg (2lb 4oz) spinach
- sea salt flakes and black pepper

1. Heat the oil in a pan over a medium heat. Add the onions with a pinch of salt and cook for 10–12 minutes until soft and starting to colour. They still want to have texture but be at that stage when they go sweet and soft. Add to a large mixing bowl with the rest of the filling ingredients except the spinach.

2. In the same pan if it is big enough, add the spinach a couple of handfuls at a time and stir to wilt. Repeat until all the spinach is wilted. Remove to a sieve over a bowl and press out as much liquid as you can. Removing and draining in batches is also fine – whatever makes it most manageable.

3. Preheat the oven to 180°C (350°F), Gas Mark 4.

4. Roughly chop through the spinach and add to the rest of the filling. Mix well, taste for seasoning and add more salt and black pepper as needed.

5. Brush your baking tin with butter. Add a sheet of filo and brush with butter. Repeat this for four more sheets. Then add the filling. Fold the overhanging filo sheets over the filling. Then brush the final two sheets with butter and lay on top of each other. Trim these to fit the tin exactly. Put the trimmings in the middle of the tin to cover any exposed filling. Lay the final sheets on top. Score the top into six sections. Add the sesame seeds in an even layer. Bake for 45–55 minutes. Remove from the oven and allow to sit for 10–15 minutes before serving.

SPINACH soup with haricot beans & goat's cheese

This relies on the aromatics in the beans to add a baseline depth to the overall dish. If using pre-cooked beans, try and find jarred or Tetra Pak versions. The beans tend to be much softer. SERVES 4

- 300g (10½oz) dried haricot beans, soaked overnight, or 660g (1lb 7oz) cooked, jarred or Tetra Pak
- 2 bay leaves
- 2 stalks of sage
- 8 small garlic cloves
- 2 tablespoons neutral oil, such as sunflower or groundnut
- 2 small onions, roughly diced
- 100ml (3½fl oz) white wine
- 600g (1lb 5oz) spinach
- 2 Crottin or small, hard individual goat's cheeses or 120g (4¼oz) other hard goat's cheese
- sea salt flakes and black pepper
- extra-virgin olive oil

1. Cover the beans and bay leaves, sage and garlic with water in a pan. Bring to a very gentle simmer and cook for 45 minutes or until soft when squeezed. Keep topping up the water to cover if needed. Once done turn off the heat. If using canned beans, I add the garlic and gently soften it in a tablespoon of oil. Then add the bay leaves and sage stalks, followed by the beans with their liquor. Heat through and then turn off the heat and set aside to infuse a little.

2. Heat the oil in a large saucepan. Add the onions and a pinch of salt. Cook gently for 8–12 minutes until soft and translucent. Add the wine and bring to a bubble. Add in the spinach and keep stirring to get the wilted leaves to the top and the top leaves to the bottom. Place a lid on and allow to steam for a minute or so, then repeat the stirring ritual. Keep everything moving until the leaves are just wilted. Turn off the heat, transfer to a blender and blitz until smooth. If the mix is a bit stuck, add a ladle of bean liquor to help everything get moving.

3. Drain the beans, reserving the cooking liquor. Remove the sage and bay leaves. Add the spinach soup to a pan to warm thorugh with salt and cracked black pepper to your liking. Loosen the mix with the bean liquor to a consistency you like. It wants to be fluid but not a swimming pool.

4. Divide the soup among bowls. Spoon over the beans and top with slices of Crottin or goat's cheese to melt in and a good drizzle of olive oil.

CAVOLO cannelloni

I started out going a couple of different directions with this recipe, but ultimately I think this is most user-friendly and best-tasting version. You can use shop-bought fresh pasta sheets if you like, but the idea is to be fairly no-nonsense. Rolling the sheets up like snails means you get lots of layers of filling and pasta – a sort of cross between cannelloni and lasagne. Play with the different elements as you please – chilli flakes in the tomato sauce work a treat. Any excess pasta trimmings I cut into strips and freeze on a tray in nests before transferring to a smaller container, then cook straight from frozen in boiling water when needed. I use various high-protein flours. Unbleached white is a good option. But I also use light brown flour or finely milled wholemeal. It is worth a play if you want more flavour and texture from your pasta. If you want a saucier version do 1.5 x the sauce amounts. SERVES 6

FOR THE PASTA
- 400g (14oz) high-protein flour
- 4 eggs
- 2 tablespoons olive oil

FOR THE FILLING
- 2 onions or 1 large shallot
- 600g (1lb 5oz) cavolo nero or kale, leaves separated from the stalks
- 500g (1lb 2oz) ricotta
- 150g (5½oz) Italian-style hard cheese, grated
- zest and juice of 2 lemons
- sea salt flakes and black pepper

FOR THE TOMATO SAUCE
- 4 tablespoons olive oil
- 4 garlic cloves, sliced
- 2 x 400g (14oz) cans plum tomatoes

1. Add the pasta ingredients to a stand mixer fitted with the dough hook. Mix for 5–7 minutes until a smooth dough is formed. You can also do this by hand; bring together the ingredients and knead for 10–15 minutes to form a smooth dough. Cover the dough with a plate or upturned bowl and allow to rest for 30 minutes.

2. Heat the olive oil in a large pan and add the onion. Cook until soft and translucent, about 8–12 minutes. Remove from the pan to a mixing bowl. Fill the pan with water, salt it and bring to a boil. Finely chop the cavolo nero stalks and leaves. Once the water is boiling, add the chopped stalks and cook for 2 minutes. Then follow with the leaves and cook for a further 2–3 minutes. I pull out a piece and eat it to check if it is soft enough. Drain well and spread out on a tray to cool.

3. To make the sauce, gently heat the oil in a medium pan and add the garlic. Once sizzling, add the tomatoes with a good pinch of salt. Break them up with a wooden spoon or a potato masher. Half-fill the cans with water and add to the pan. Bubble away for 10–15 minutes. Blend or leave coarser to your liking. Check the seasoning and set aside.

4. Mix the ricotta with 100g (3½oz) of the hard cheese, the zest of both lemons plus the juice of one, along with some salt and pepper. Add the cavolo nero. Taste and add more lemon juice and seasoning if needed.

5. Add half the tomato sauce to your baking dish – I use a 35 x 22cm (14 x 8½in) high-sided roasting tray. Then start rolling out the pasta into strips. It wants to be about the width of your tray, so mine are 12cm (4½in). Cut into rough 12cm (4½in) squares. You want to end up with 16 rough squares. Spread a good dollop of filling onto each square and roughly spread out. Roll them up into long snail shapes and add to the roasting tray in a line as you go. Top with the remaining sauce and finish with the remaining hard cheese. Bake for 30–40 minutes in the oven until bubbling. Serve with a green salad and red wine.

Black pepper tofu with *SPINACH*

I didn't cook tofu enough at home. This recipe changed that. Make the tofu this way and use for other dishes. It is so crisp and crunchy, giving way to a soft centre. One of the hurdles with tofu can be getting flavours to permeate. I find this method combats that by sticking a decent amount of black pepper properly to the edges. It adds a warming spice and keeps the tofu interesting.

SERVES 4

- 2–3 tablespoons oil, plus extra for deep-frying, I use sunflower
- 2 onions, sliced
- 80g (2¾oz) cornflour
- 20g (¾oz) freshly crushed black pepper, use a small blender for speed
- 10g (¼oz) sea salt flakes
- 450g (1lb) firm tofu, drained and cut into 2–3cm (¾–1¼in) cubes
- 2–4 chillies, finely sliced
- 800g (1lb 12oz) spinach
- 1 tablespoon mild curry powder
- 1 small red onion, finely sliced
- cooked rice, oat groats, barley, spelt and/or roti or naan of your choosing, to serve

1. Heat the oil in a large pan over a medium heat. Add the onions and cook gently for 8–10 minutes until starting to colour.

2. Heat a large, high-sided frying pan with about 2cm (¾in) depth of oil or use a deep-fat fryer if you have one. Mix the cornflour, pepper and salt together. Add the tofu cubes and toss to coat evenly. Check the oil with a thermometer and when at 180°C (350°F) you are good to go. Working in batches, carefully place the tofu into the pan and fry for 1–2 minutes on each side until golden and crispy. Work in batches not to drop the oil temperature too much.

3. Remove with a slotted spoon to a paper-lined plate or a sieve over a mixing bowl. Sprinkle with a final flourish of salt. When the last batch is approaching being done, add the chillies and allow them to sizzle and crisp slightly. Drain them all and mix through the rest of the tofu.

4. Meanwhile, add a good pinch of salt, the curry powder and spinach to the cooked onions. Cook to wilt the spinach. Arrange on a platter or serving dish and lay the chilli and tofu on top. Finish with the sliced red onion and serve with your grain and/or bread of choice.

BRUSSELS
& beetroot slaw

The kefir in this recipe brings everything together with a delicious tang. If you don't have celery leaves, no bother, sub in parsley or chervil. Feel free to use this dish where you please – as a topping for soups or stews, in cheese sandwiches or just alongside a pie. Crunchy and sweet with a lovely sourness to balance, it goes well with most things. SERVES 4 AS A SALAD OR 8 AS A TOPPING

- 400g (14oz) beetroot, boiled until cooked through, peeled and cooled
- 500g (1lb 2oz) Brussels sprouts, trimmed and outer leaves removed, shredded
- 5 spring onions, finely sliced
- leaves from a head of celery
- 200ml (7fl oz) kefir, buttermilk or natural yogurt
- juice of 1 lemon, or more to taste
- sea salt flakes and black pepper

1. Dice the peeled beetroot into roughly 1cm (½in) cubes, then add to the shredded Brussels. Follow with the rest of the ingredients and stir well to combine. Don't overdo it otherwise everything will turn pink, which is no bad thing, but it is nice to see the different elements.

2. Adjust the salt and lemon juice to taste. Serve as is as a salad or spoon onto a lentil dhal as a crunchy, chunky raita of sorts.

Roast *BRUSSELS SPROUTS* with whipped tahini, spicy tomato chutney & crouton crumbs

Creamy, crunchy, spicy, caramelized. Ticking all the right boxes so far. This dish is a lovely balance of textures and flavours that elevates the humble Brussels sprout to new heights. All the elements can be prepped ahead and then assembled when you are ready to serve. The Brussels take no time to cook. I just love roast Brussels sprouts – crispy and caramelized outsides with soft steamed centres. I like to undercook the onion and chilli in the chutney a bit so it retains a crunch and a freshness, cooked through but not fully softened.

SERVES 4–6 AS A STARTER OR SIDE

- 100–150g (3½–5½oz) bread, roughly cubed, I use sourdough, but any good-quality bread works
- 7–8 tablespoons olive oil, plus extra to serve
- 1 onion, roughly diced
- 1 celery stick, sliced
- 2 red chillies, diced
- 400g (14oz) Brussels sprouts
- 400g (14oz) can plum tomatoes
- 40g (1½oz) honey or unrefined sugar
- juice of 1 lemon
- 150g (5½oz) tahini
- sea salt flakes

1. Preheat the oven to 200°C (400°F), Gas Mark 6. Toss the bread in 2–3 tablespoons of oil. Add to a baking tray and toast in the oven for 10–12 minutes until golden. Blitz to crumbs in a blender, or leave whole or hand cut if you prefer.

2. Meanwhile, add 2 tablespoons of oil to a medium pan over a medium heat. Add the onion, celery and chillies with a pinch of salt and cook for 5–7 minutes. Add the tomatoes. Half-fill the can with water and add to the pan. Bring to a simmer and bubble away for 15 minutes until thickened. It still wants to be loose but not watery. Add the honey and check if it needs more salt. Set aside.

3. Increase the oven temperature to 220°C (425°F), Gas Mark 7. Using the same tray as the croutons, brush out any remaining crumbs and add the Brussels with 3 tablespoons of oil and a good pinch of salt. Roast for 12 minutes. You want to roast them quickly, getting colour on the outside and cooking through without going overly soft in the middle. If they need a bit more, keep them in a minute or two longer. Feel free to give the tray a shake once or twice to aid them in cooking evenly.

4. Meanwhile, mix the lemon juice with the tahini and trickle in a few tablespoons of cold water. Keep working it with a whisk and adding water until you get a smooth consistency which holds its shape. If it gets too loose, just add a spoon or two of tahini and combine it to help firm up the mix.

5. Spoon the tahini mixture onto plates or a serving dish, followed by the Brussels sprouts. Then dot around the tomato chutney. You made not need it all, see how you go. Finish with the crouton crumbs and a drizzle of oil.

Pikelets with pickled *CABBAGE*

Yes I appreciate these aren't really a green. The recipe was originally something else that changed, but I wanted to keep these in. They are a fairly quick and easy way to complete a plate of food, adding substance to a ploughman's lunch or alongside salads or other lighter offerings. I get these going first thing when I come down in the morning to allow the yeast to start getting to work if having them for breakfast. They work just as well with all water also. I tend to make a full batch, then put any left over in the toaster the next day to reheat and crisp slightly. I used to always get pikelets from Betty's in York. A good crumpet is a thing of beauty, but I find pikelets a little more versatile. For the pickled red cabbage, follow the ingredients and method for the pickled cucumber on page 150, replacing the cucumbers with a finely shredded head of cabbage. Store the pickled cabbage in the fridge for up to 3 months. When adding the pickling liquor I stick a funnel down into the cabbage and fill from there, it helps me be slightly less messy. MAKES 12

- 500g (1lb 2oz) light brown wheat flour, other flours or a blend also work fine
- 5g (⅛oz) fast action dried yeast
- 350ml (12fl oz) milk, you can use plant-based milk
- 350ml (12fl oz) hot water
- 2 tablespoons oil, I use sunflower but any works
- 2 good pinches of salt

  TO SERVE (optional)
- jam and butter
- honey
- cheese
- pickled cabbage (see intro)
- apple or pears, sliced

1. Mix the flour and yeast together. Then add the water to the milk. You can use all water if you are out of milk. Check the temperature if you have a thermometer or test it against your lip. You don't want it much past 26–28°C (79–82°F). It should be warm but not overly hot. The temperature will drop when introduced to the flour, but you don't want to over-stress the yeast. Add the oil and salt and mix everything together to form a smooth batter. Leave covered for 30–60 minutes until bubbling and doubled in size. The longer, the better, to be honest.

2. Heat a frying pan over a low–medium heat and grease it lightly with oil. Add the batter a ladle at a time. (Or make smaller ones if you like.) Let down with a little water if the mix is too thick. Once the bubbles begin to pop on top and the edges look set, flip the pikelets over and cook through on the other side.

3. Serve in any way you see fit – sweet or savoury. With eggs and pickled chillies in the morning, or topped with spinach and cheddar and placed under the grill for a light lunch. But as I say they reheat really well in the toaster so can be made ahead.

End of summer *PAELLA*

I often make this for when people come over toward the end of the summer. I like that you set it up and trust in the cooking so you can relax and be with people. I'm not a massive fan of the flavour of saffron, but I think that comes from people overusing it. A small, subtle pinch goes a very long way. Be judicious. Soaking a pinch of saffron in a tablespoon of boiling water and adding to the blender when making the aioli is another nice way of getting the flavour in the dish. That way people can add as much or little as they like. If you want to avoid the oven, finish cooking over a low flame. Spread 300–400g (10½–14oz) of baby-leaf spinach over the top. This acts like a lid and helps the paella cook evenly. Test to see when the rice is cooked. You can also add spinach to the oven version when it comes out, just let it wilt over the top for a minute or so. SERVES 8

- 9 tablespoons olive oil
- 2 aubergines, tops removed, cut into 2cm (¾in) dice
- pinch of saffron strands (optional)
- 1.2 litres (2½ pints) hot vegetable stock
- 2 onions, diced
- 3 garlic cloves, sliced
- 2 courgettes, cut into rough 1cm (½in) dice
- 2 peppers, stalks and most of the seeds removed, diced
- 1 heaped tablespoon sweet paprika
- 300g (10½oz) cherry tomatoes, halved or grated if large
- 500g (1lb 2oz) paella rice, bomba and Calasparra are the most common
- 250ml (9fl oz) sherry, vin jaune or white wine
- 30g (1oz) parsley, finely chopped
- sea salt flakes

TO SERVE
- aioli
- lemon wedges

1. Preheat the oven to 200°C (400°F), Gas Mark 6. Heat 4 tablespoons of oil in a large pan that will accommodate everything over a medium-high heat. A 36cm (14in) paella pan works a treat for obvious reasons. Make sure the pan fits in the oven before you start. Add the aubergines and a good pinch of salt. Cook, stirring and turning the aubergines once they begin to colour. Keep cooking for 5–7 minutes until they are well coloured and soft. Remove from the pan.

2. Mix the saffron into the stock if using. Add the remaining 2 tablespoons of oil to the pan with the onions over a medium heat. Cook for 5–7 minutes until beginning to soften. Add the garlic, courgettes and peppers. Cook for a further 2 minutes. Add the paprika and tomatoes, stir and add the rice, followed by the wine. Try not to stir too much. Add the stock and the aubergines. Give everything a little prod to distribute evenly, bring to a bubble on the stove for 2–3 minutes to make it less fluid when transferring to the oven, then carefully place the pan in the oven. Cook for 10–15 minutes until the liquid has evaporated and the rice is just tender.

3. Sprinkle over the chopped parsley and serve with aioli and lemon wedges.

Battered *COURGETTES* with lemon & chive yogurt

Another dish that instantly transports me back to being on holiday. I do love this dish as it showcases courgettes so well. Paired with a creamy sauce, they are absolutely heavenly. Close your eyes while eating them and play a track of sounds of the sea lapping gently at a sandy beach. You could easily be on a Greek island. Try to get firm, smallish courgettes. These should have less seeds and contain less water so won't go mushy when cooked.

SERVES 4–6 AS A STARTER

- 500–600g (1lb 2oz–1lb 5oz) courgettes
- 200g (7oz) plain flour
- 50g (2oz) cornflour
- 1 teaspoon baking powder
- 300–400ml (10½–14fl oz) sparkling water
- sunflower oil, for frying (about 1.5–2 litres/2⅔– 3½ pints if using a pan)
- sea salt flakes
- 300g (10½oz) natural yogurt or soured cream
- 25g (1oz) chives, finely chopped
- zest and juice of 2 lemons, plus wedges to serve

1. Cut each courgette into quarters lengthways. If the centres are fluffy and not very firm, lay them on a cut side and run a knife down the length to remove them. Cut each quarter in half down its length so each courgette ends up being divided into eighths.

2. Mix the flours, baking powder and sparkling water together with a good pinch of salt. Don't overwork the batter, just gently bring everything together.

3. Either in a fryer or a high-sided casserole pan, heat a 5–6cm (2–2½in) depth of oil to 180°C (350°F), or when some batter dropped in it sizzles immediately and turns golden after 10–15 seconds.

4. Mix the yogurt with the chives, lemon juice to taste and salt.

5. Drop a few sections of courgette into the batter. Lift out one at a time, holding just the very end. Allow most of the batter to run off and gently place in the oil. Fry for 1–2 minutes until golden and crisp. Remove to a sieve over a bowl to drain well. Check one of the first ones to see if the courgette is cooked through. If so, repeat as you are. Otherwise, keep them in a little longer. Season well with salt.

6. Serve with lemon zest scattered over the courgettes and the yogurt dip and lemon wedges on the side.

SPINACH roulade

If you look up the definition of kitsch in the dictionary there could well be a picture of spinach roulade. That being said, the flavours are all solid and work extremely well together. I was going to go the traditional rolled roulade route, but this way of constructing the layers seemed simpler and less stressful to me. You can tidy up the edges and have quite a smart and impressive-looking dish. The mixture will roll if you are rooted firmly in the presentation past. This makes a great lunch served simply with some buttered new potatoes. Use different ratios of the cheeses to your taste. SERVES 6, MORE IF USING AS A SIDE OR CANAPÉ

- 100g (3½oz) unsalted butter
- 100g (3½oz) light brown flour, other flour works fine
- 800ml (1⅓ pints) whole milk
- 600g (1lb 5oz) spinach
- 4 eggs, separated
- 150g (5½oz) good quality cream cheese
- 150g (5½oz) ricotta
- 150g (5½oz) soft goat's cheese
- zest and juice of 1–2 lemons
- sea salt flakes amd black pepper

1. In a pan, melt the butter and flour together over a medium-low heat. Cook out the flour for 2–3 minutes until golden and aromatic. Add the milk a quarter at a time, stirring well with a whisk to fully incorporate. Cook for 5–10 minutes until the sauce thickens and is coming away from the sides of the pan.

2. Preheat the oven to 200°C (400°F), Gas Mark 6. Line two identical trays with greaseproof paper. I use 25 x 35cm (10 x 14in) ones.

3. In a pan of salted boiling water, blanch the spinach for a few seconds. Drain and refresh in iced water. Once cool, squeeze out any excess water. Roughly chop and add to a blender with a good pinch of salt and the white sauce. Blend until smooth. Allow to cool to room temperature for 30 minutes.

4. In a separate mixing bowl, whisk the egg whites with a pinch of salt until they hold their shape of soft peaks. Fold the egg yolks in to the spinach mix to incorporate them. Fold the spinach mixture into the egg whites, trying not to knock out too much air. Divide the mixture between the trays and bake for 10–15 minutes until starting to colour on top and set. The tray on the bottom shelf may need an extra 5 minutes at the top of the oven.

5. Remove the spinach sheets from the trays and allow to cool on wire racks. Mix the cream cheese, ricotta and goat's cheese together with the lemon zest and juice, as well as salt and pepper to taste.

6. Cut each spinach sheet in half. Spread the cheese filling onto three pieces. Then stack them on top of one another, finishing with the layer without any cheese. Trim the edges to neaten them up. Clean the knife each time you cut to help keep the edges sharp. Cut into the portion sizes you require.

BOBBY BEANS with lemon ricotta & basil

This marks the beginning of summer for me. When beans start to show up as spring transitions into summer, and you can start eating meals outside again. Any kind of beans are good for this – runner beans, broad beans, a mix of colours of bobby beans. SERVES 4

- 450g (1lb) bobby beans, stalk ends trimmed
- 250g (9oz) ricotta
- zest and juice of 2 lemons
- 15g (½oz) basil, a mix of types is good
- 2–3 tablespoons extra-virgin olive oil
- sea salt flakes and black pepper

1. Blanch the beans in well-salted water for 3–5 minutes until just tender with a little resistance. Drain and place in an ice bath. Chill for 5 minutes or until completely cool. Drain fully.

2. In a small bowl, mix the ricotta with a pinch of salt and half the lemon juice. Taste and add more lemon juice to your desired level. Spread on a serving plate. Mix the beans with the basil, lemon zest and 2 tablespoons of oil. Add on top of the ricotta with a few grinds of black pepper. A final sprinkle of salt and a drizzle of the remaining oil is always good.

GREEN polenta

This is perfect just on its own, topped with healthy amounts of grated cheese and good oil. I stick my hard cheese in the food processor and pulse until it resembles breadcrumbs. I like the texture doing it this way, as there is more bite. Fried sage is also most welcome. It reheats really well, just add a splash of water to the saucepan. Try to break up the polenta as much as possible. Then, over a really low heat with a lid on, let it revive, stirring occasionally. You can use other greens in place of the cavolo nero – kale is an easy substitute, but broccoli also works well. If you want to make this into a more substantial offering roast sections of squash or pumpkin, lightly dressed in olive oil and salt, in the oven for 25–35 minutes at 180°C (350°F), Gas Mark 4 until tender and caramelized.

SERVES 6 AS A STARTER OR SIDE

- 500g (1lb 2oz) cavolo nero
- 5 garlic cloves
- 2–3 tablespoons extra-virgin olive oil, plus extra to serve
- 250g (9oz) quick-cook polenta
- sea salt flakes and black pepper

TO SERVE
- roast squash or pumpkin (optional, see intro)
- grated hard cheese
- 1 teaspoon chilli flakes (optional)

1. Set a pan of water on to boil with a healthy pinch of salt. Separate the stalks from the cavolo nero. Roughly chop. Roughly chop the leaves. Add the stalks to the water with the garlic and cook for 2 minutes. Add the leaves and blanch for a further 2–3 minutes. I pull out a piece and taste to see if it is tender enough. When it is, drain and add to a blender with the oil. Blend to a smooth purée. Use some cooking water to get it moving if you need.

2. Using the same pan, bring 1 litre (2 pints) of water to the boil. The same water from blanching the cavolo nero is fine. Pour in the polenta in one stream while stirring with a whisk to help avoid lumps. Keep stirring with a whisk to avoid any parts clumping together. Cook the polenta for 5 minutes until it is cooked through and beginning to bubble like lava.

3. Stir the cavolo nero purée into the polenta to completely combine. Check the seasoning and add salt and pepper to taste.

4. Spoon onto plates and serve with a generous splash of extra-virgin olive oil and hard cheese grated over the top and chilli flakes, if you like.

CHARD with walnuts & blue cheese

Showcasing beautiful chard with a few simple support characters. Combining three of the best ingredients around in one salad is a win in my book. The trick is getting the stalks to absorb the vinegar to get them to the semi-quick pickle stage. Deliciously moreish. This goes very well with the fennel and potato gratin on page 112, leaving out the blue cheese as the gratin is already fairly cheesy. SERVES 4 AS A SIDE OR 2 AS A LIGHT LUNCH WITH A GRAIN OR BREAD

- 100g (3½oz) walnut halves
- 800g (1lb 12oz) rainbow chard, Swiss is fine also
- 2-3 tablespoons red wine vinegar
- 2 tablespoons extra-virgin olive oil
- 100-150g (3½-5½oz) blue cheese, I use Stilton, but any works, roughly crumbled
- 15g (½oz) dill, leaves picked
- sea salt flakes and black pepper

1. Preheat the oven to 180°C (350°F), Gas Mark 4. Toast the walnuts in the oven for 10-12 minutes until golden.

2. Put a pan of salted water on to boil. Separate the chard stalks from the leaves. If the chard stalks are really chunky, split them down the middle lengthways. Blanch the leaves for 1-2 minutes until just tender. Lay out on a tray or platter to cool. Blanch the stalks for 2-3 minutes until cooked but still with a little bite. They take longer if they are larger.

3. Slice along the stalks on the diagonal to get 3-4cm (1¼-1½in) sections. Add to a mixing bowl with the vinegar and oil. Season well with salt and black pepper. Allow to sit for 5-10 minutes.

4. When ready to serve, arrange the leaves spread out on a serving dish. Spoon over the stalks. Add the walnuts, gently crushing them in your hand as you go, followed by the cheese and the dill.

Roast
CAULIFLOWER tacos

Taco night is always one of the best nights for us. The buzz of excitement around the table is palpable. Everyone loves piling in and building their own tacos however they please. You can replace the cabbage with the pickled cabbage from page 132. I like making fresh corn tortillas. You can by all means use shop-bought ones – there are some very good options these days. But I wanted to find a quick and easy alternative to use instead. These lentil versions, pancakes essentially, fill that need. They are quick enough for a breakfast as well. Scrambled egg breakfast tacos are a splendid way to start the day. SERVES 4

- 6–7 tablespoons oil, I use sunflower, plus extra for frying
- 1 tablespoon chilli powder or hot paprika
- 1 tablespoon ground coriander
- 2 medium cauliflowers (about 1kg/2lb 4oz), broken into 2–3cm (¾ –1¼in) pieces, stalk and leaves cut same size
- 1 onion, finely diced
- 15–25g (½–1oz) coriander, roughly chopped
- 5–6 limes, 3 cut into quarters
- 250g (9oz) split red lentils
- 400ml (14fl oz) water
- 150g (5oz) crème fraîche
- 75g (2⅔oz) mayonnaise (see page 12 for homemade plant-based version)
- ½ small head of red or white cabbage or Hispi works, shredded thinly
- pickled chillies, either good ones from a jar or use the recipe on page 90
- sea salt flakes

1. Preheat the oven to 200°C (400°F), Gas Mark 6. In a mixing bowl, combine 4–5 tablespoons of the oil with the chilli powder and ground coriander, plus a good pinch of salt. Add the cauliflower and toss to coat well with the spiced oil. Lay out onto baking trays so the cauliflower isn't cramped. Use two trays if needed.

2. Roast the cauliflower in the oven for 20 minutes. Turn the pieces of cauliflower and continue to cook for a further 10–15 minutes. Once the cauliflower is golden, soft inside and has a good caramelization on its edges, remove from the oven.

3. Meanwhile, mix the onion with the coriander, a good pinch of salt and the juice of 2–3 of the limes to taste. Set aside.

4. In a high-speed blender, blitz the lentils with the water, a good pinch of salt and 2 healthy tablespoons of oil. Run it for a good couple of minutes to get the mixture completely smooth.

5. Heat a frying pan oven a medium-low heat and lightly oil it. The mixture is enough for 12 pancakes. Pour in your first amount of mix and spread out to roughly 14–15cm (5½–6in) with the back of the ladle. Cook for 1–2 minutes until the bubbles that have formed on top are popping, the edges look set and cooked through and the pancake releases from the pan. Flip and cook any raw batter on the top side. Once cooked, place the pancakes in a sealed container so they can steam. This helps keep them malleable. Repeat until all the mixture is used up.

6. Mix the crème fraîche and mayonnaise together with a pinch of salt. Place in a small bowl. Add to a platter or a tray with the cabbage, pickled chillies, lime wedges and the onion coriander salsa. Followed by the cauliflower when cooked.

CUCUMBERS CARROTS & SALADS

We, as a family, must make a not insignificant dent in the world's **CUCUMBER** supplies. When in season we easily go through one or two while cooking before we sit down to eat. Simply as slices, maybe sprinkled with some sea salt or layered with a thin slice of Cheddar cheese. It helps keep everyone's hunger at bay while waiting for the food to cook. But is just such a wonderful burst of freshness that you can feel cooling your blood and charging you up. Make sure you pickle loads to enjoy them in a different guise over the winter months.

Pickled *CUCUMBER*

These are kind of my no-nonsense version of bread and butter pickles. Do use this as a template and swap in and out spices to suit the mood or cuisine. Add ½ teaspoon of ground turmeric to the mix to get colour and flavour. I think the little touch of fennel just adds the right note. I keep these on repeat in the fridge door. Once they are finished, I refresh the mix and reuse it. Strain the liquid, add a splash more vinegar, a scant teaspoon of sugar or honey and a good pinch of salt, then heat and repeat.

MAKES 2 X 1 LITRE (1¾ PINT) JARS

1. In a saucepan, toast the fennel seeds until aromatic. Add the vinegar, water, sugar, salt and bring to a simmer.

2. Add the cucumbers and shallots to your jars. Plastic containers also works well.

3. Pour the liquid into the jars and seal the lids. I leave out on the work surface for couple of hours or so to reduce the temperature a bit. Then put in the fridge for up to 3 months.

- 1 heaped tablespoon fennel seeds
- 500ml (18fl oz) cider vinegar
- 500ml (18fl oz) water
- 50g (1¾oz) unrefined sugar or honey
- 8g (¼oz) sea salt
- 2–3 cucumbers (about 800g/1lb 12oz), sliced into 3–5mm (1/8–¼in) thick rounds
- 2–3 banana shallots or 1 small onion, finely sliced

CUCUMBERS in cream

I had this dish when visiting the winemaker Catherine Hannoun in Jura, France. Cucumbers picked fresh from her garden moments before. A perfect summer dish. Great as part of a summer meal or as an intro with some crusty baguette. I put the cucumber skins in a jug of water to infuse. SERVES 4–6

- 800g (1lb 12oz) cucumbers (about 2 medium)
- 1 garlic clove
- 125ml (4½fl oz) double cream
- 15g (½oz) chives, garlic chives or chervil, finely chopped
- a splash of white wine vinegar
- sea salt flakes and black pepper

1. Peel the cucumbers and slice them finely. Add a good pinch of salt and mix well. Set aside for an hour or two. Give them a mix when you remember.

2. When ready to serve, cut the garlic clove in half and rub the cut side around your serving bowl. Drain the liquid from the cucumbers and give them a squeeze to get rid of any extra liquid. Discard the liquid and add the cucumbers to the mixing bowl along with the cream, herbs and a touch of vinegar. Mix well to combine. Taste and add more vinegar if it needs it. The salt level should be enough but add more if it needs it, plus a cracking of black pepper to finish.

Chilled *CUCUMBER* & herb soup

Add the cucumber peelings to a water jug to let them infuse, preferably in the fridge overnight, so not to waste food and you get an energy drink which is packed with electrolytes. This soup keeps well in the fridge for a couple of days. It is best served very chilled. A lovely refreshing summer starter, it can also be served in small glasses if you are at more of an informal barbecue and not sat around a table. Feel free to play with the ratios of herbs and which ones you want to include. Do go with your personal favourites. SERVES 4 OR MORE IF SERVING IN SMALL GLASSES

- 1kg (2lb 4oz) cucumbers (about 3 medium), peeled and deseeded
- 300g (10½oz) natural yogurt
- 3 spring onions, roughly chopped
- 1 garlic clove or ½ teaspoon garlic powder
- 20g (¾oz) dill
- 15g (½oz) parsley, tough stalks removed
- 10g (¼oz) tarragon, leaves picked
- 10g (¼oz) chives
- 1–2 tablespoons white wine vinegar, or to taste
- sea salt flakes and black pepper

TO SERVE
- a handful of extra herbs, such as basil, chervil, tarragon, chives, dill or any soft herbs you like
- extra-virgin olive oil

1. Add the ingredients to the blender with 1 tablespoon of the vinegar and a healthy pinch of salt. Blend until very smooth. Go for a couple of minutes and then a minute or so more.

2. Taste the soup and add more salt or vinegar according to your taste. Go a little heavier than usual as the soup is served cold, so the punch will be muted a little.

3. Serve topped with a scattering of herbs, olive oil and a good grind of black pepper.

BANH MI

I came across this combination of peanut butter and fried egg in Hoi An at Banh Mi Phuong. It was one of those moments that makes you take a step back and appreciate that the sum of these simple ingredients is something just so outrageously delicious. The balance of the fried egg, crunchy sweet peanut butter, sharp pickles and fresh salad is masterful. Crusty baguettes are a must. If in season and at peak levels of tastiness, thin slices of cucumber and tomato are welcome, and what was in the sandwich when I originally had it. But the most important thing is the peanut butter and egg combo. I like a mix of deep, rich chilli oil and bright, fresh sriracha sauce, for a double chilli hit. If making these for a crowd, I like having the toppings set out on the table, then all I have to do is fry the eggs and brush in the peanut butter, essentially locking in the main part of the sandwich and then letting everyone finish it as they please. SERVES 1

- 1 tablespoon sunflower oil
- 2 eggs
- sea salt flakes
- 1–2 tablespoons crunchy peanut butter
- ⅓ baguette, cut most of the way through and opened up
- 1 spring onion, finely sliced
- a few slices of cucumber, if in season
- pickled carrots and daikon (see page 160)
- couple of sprigs of coriander
- your favourite chilli oil and/or chilli sauce
- pickled chillis from page 90

1. Heat the oil in a small frying pan over a high heat. Crack the eggs into a glass or jug with a pinch of salt. Run a fork through them 2–3 times to break the yolks and marble the yolk and white together a little.

2. Spread the peanut butter onto one cut side of the baguette.

3. Add the eggs to the pan. Allow to sizzle and bubble for 30 seconds. With the fork or a spatula, pull in the edge of the omelette to the centre a couple of times to allow very fluid egg to come into contact with the pan surface. After another 30 seconds or so, carefully flip over to cook the top side. Take off the heat as the residual heat in the pan will be enough to finish. Wait for a further 20–30 seconds and add to the baguette.

4. Serve piled up with spring onion, cucumber, if in season, pickled carrots and daikon, coriander and lots of chilli oil and/or sauce and pickled chillies.

Smacked
CUCUMBER salad

Whenever I see this dish on the menu at a Chinese restaurant I order it without fail. I love the slight variations in the way it is prepared and served. It is most welcome at the table in any version. I didn't have toasted sesame oil once when making it at home, so opted for using tahini instead to get the sesame flavour. It works really well, the creaminess balances perfectly with the refreshing cucumber and the heat of the chilli. Using sesame oil with the tahini adds a double whack of sesame flavour here. But by all means try it without the tahini if you are pairing it with something else a bit fatty. Adding toasted sesame seeds is also very pleasing. SERVES 4-6

- 60g (2¼oz) light tahini
- 1½ tablespoons toasted sesame oil
- 1½ tablespoons rice wine vinegar
- 1 tablespoon light soy sauce
- 2 garlic cloves, minced, or
  1 teaspoon garlic powder
- 3 spring onions, thinly sliced
- 800g (1lb 12oz) cucumbers
  (about 2 medium)
- 2 tablespoons of your favourite
  chilli oil
- sea salt flakes

1. In a mixing bowl big enough to accommodate everything, add the tahini, sesame oil, vinegar, soy sauce and garlic. Mix well to combine. Taste and add any more of each element you think may be lacking. Add a pinch of salt and the spring onions. Mix to incorporate.

2. Trim the tough stalks ends off the cucumbers. Then with a cleaver, wide knife or a small saucepan, give the cucumbers a solid smacking along their lengths. Invigoration rather than decimation is key here. Otherwise, the walls get a lot of the cucumbers intended for the mixing bowl. You are looking to break them apart a bit and essentially get the juices going.

3. Cut along the crushed lengths on a diagonal about 2–3cm (¾ –1¼in) apart. Add to the dressing and mix well to coat everything.

4. Once the dressed cucumbers are on their serving plate, drizzle liberally with your favourite chilli oil.

I don't tend to do too much to **CARROTS** these days, favouring their fresh crunch above all else. I grate and add to salads or in a batter for breakfast fritters. I always try and keep a bunch or two in the fridge to snack on, reaching for them with my son instead of too much fruit a lot of the time. They are very good for your teeth health apparently, like a natural toothbrush. Or just use as a brilliant vessel to transport dips into your mouth.

Pickled *CARROTS* & daikon

I like the uniformity of using a mandolin. There is something so satisfying about the same julienne or matchstick shape. That being said, by all means dice, slice or matchstick by hand with a knife. Also grating on a box grater is fine. It will get you to a similar destination, just a different texture. If a mandolin is scary, the handheld peelers with grating attachments are another good option. Also, food processors have grating attachments that will do julienne matchsticks if you have one. This is another quick pickle that my son absolutely loves, so I keep a large jar in the fridge door. As soon as he could open the fridge door, he would go and stand there pointing at the jar for me to get him a handful to snack on. Stuff in sandwiches, especially the banh mi on page 157. Have with noodles, on a plate of ploughman's, with sausage and mash – just about anywhere the natural sweetness of the carrot and the balance of the vinegar cuts the richness of other foods.
MAKES 1 X 1.5 LITRE (2 ⅔ PINT) JAR

- 450g (1lb) carrots, washed and stalk ends trimmed
- 450g (1lb) daikon, washed and stalk ends trimmed
- 300ml (10fl oz) rice vinegar
- 300ml (10fl oz) water
- 3 star anise
- 1 heaped tablespoon coriander seeds
- 50g (1¾oz) unrefined sugar or honey
- 10g (¼oz) sea salt

1. Mandolin, chop or grate your carrots and daikon. Add to the jar.

2. In a saucepan, bring the vinegar, water, spices, sugar and salt to a simmer. Stir to dissolve the sugar.

3. Pour the liquid into the jar and seal the lid. I leave out on the work surface for couple of hours or so, then put in the fridge for up to 3 months.

4. You can also refresh the pickling liquor for reuse. Strain the liquid, add a splash more vinegar, a scant teaspoon of sugar or honey and a good pinch of salt, then heat and repeat.

The best meals are those that include a leafy **SALAD** course. There is something about having a plate piled high with dressed leafy greens to bring the savoury side of things to a close. It is definitely worth making a jar of dressing and keeping in the fridge to help speed this up when it comes to mealtimes. Equally, any fresh, crunchy, acid-spiked plate of food that fits loosely in the salad grouping at a meal is a win in my book.

Summer *SALAD* with feta

This salad obviously leans heavily on Greek influences, especially crowning it with a block of feta. I love a traditional Greek salad but have added other elements over time. It is a salad that I tend to make whenever I'm away from home and has evolved over time and trips as it depends on what's available in the market. It is always such a joy to get the freshest produce straight from the market, still warm from the sun. I could eat this every day for lunch in the summertime. It is great at a barbeque. SERVES 4 AS A SIDE OR STARTER

- 3 tablespoons red wine vinegar
- 4 tablespoons extra-virgin olive oil, plus extra to serve
- 1 cucumber
- 1 red onion, or Tropea onion is milder, roughly sliced
- 6 ripe tomatoes, cut into quarters
- 1 green pepper, deseeded and roughly chopped
- 150g (5½oz) radishes, sliced, if the leaves are in good condition, they can go in as well
- about 75g (2½ oz) Greek black olives, pitted and torn in half
- a good handful of basil leaves
- 2 tablespoons dried oregano
- 200g (7oz) feta
- sea salt flakes and black pepper

1. In a large mixing bowl, combine the vinegar and olive oil with a pinch of salt and a few grinds of black pepper.

2. Cut the cucumber into diagonal cross-sections along its length, rotating it a half turn each cut so you get jagged chunks. Add to the mixing bowl along with the onion, tomatoes, green pepper, radishes and olives.

3. Give everything a good mix. Add the basil leaves and most of the oregano, saving some to go on top of the feta. Check the seasoning and add more salt if needed, keeping in mind the feta is pretty salty.

4. Arrange on a platter or serving bowl. Top with the feta, the remaining sprinkle of oregano, a final drizzle of oil and serve.

Quick crunchy working lunch *SALAD*

This is my usual working lunch in varying forms. Fresh and bright, it has enough substance to keep you going through the afternoon without sending you to sleep. Crucially it also takes moments to assemble. Try different beans, swap in or add different veg according to what you have and your tastes. It is a very good platform for great olive oil and special vinegars. You can make a single serving using one can of beans, drained. Just roughly halve the other ingredients. SERVES 2

- 660g (1lb 7½oz) jar red kidney or black beans, 2 x 400g (14oz) tins work as well, drained
- 1 fennel bulb, finely sliced
- 1–2 peppers, deseeded and sliced
- 1–2 small carrots, topped and finely sliced
- 1 small red onion, finely sliced
- 1–2 jalapeños or other chillies, deseeded if you prefer, sliced
- handful of soft herbs, such as dill, coriander, basil, chervil, finely chopped
- zest and juice of 1 lemon
- 3–4 tablespoons best olive oil
- 2–3 tablespoons red wine vinegar, to taste
- sea salt flakes and black pepper

1. Combine everything in large mixing bowl. Toss well to combine. Taste and add more vinegar, lemon juice, salt and pepper to your taste.

Green *SALAD*

I make a version of this dish fairly often as my son loves it, especially with fennel, which is probably his favourite vegetable, but also try cucumber if you have it. It has Ukrainian overtones with the dill and the sour dressing, which my Ukrainian wife approves of. It is essentially a very good way to chomp down lots of fresh, crunchy salad with any meal. Please do play around with the ingredients as this is just a rough template. Mint leaves, chervil or parsley work very well as alternatives, or try adding some fruit like pear or apple. You could easily use this as a burger or wrap filling with falafels or koftes. SERVES 4 AS A STARTER OR SIDE

- 75–150g (2½–5½oz) buttermilk or natural yogurt
- 2 tablespoons capers, chopped if large
- 25g (1oz) dill, finely chopped, stalks and all
- 3 tablespoons extra-virgin olive oil
- 3 spring onions, finely sliced
- 1 kohlrabi, peeled if it is bigger and tougher, or 1 fennel bulb, or both
- 2 baby gem lettuce, roots trimmed and leaves separated
- sea salt flakes and black pepper
- crusty bread, to serve

1. In a large bowl, combine half the buttermilk, the capers, dill, oil, spring onions, a pinch of salt and a good couple grinds of black pepper. Mix to combine.

2. Finely slice the kohlrabi. I like to cut it in half and then lay it on the cut side. Then slice as thinly as I can get within reason along the length to form fairly thin sheets.

3. Add the kohlrabi to the dressing. Toss to combine well.

4. Follow with the lettuce leaves and mix well. Taste a bit and add more buttermilk, salt, pepper or oil as you see fit. Serve with crusty bread to mop up the salty sour dressing.

SWEETCORN salad

This is one of those dishes that puts a smile on your face. I make this salad a lot when we are in Ukraine as there is so much sweetcorn around in the summer. A bit of a Tex-Mex vibe going on. When I made this for the photo I left the platter on the table ready for dinner after I had finished taking the picture. I came back a while later to find my son just helping himself to fistfuls of it. He was barely high enough to reach, let alone see. He was also taking turns with his little baby seal toy, which he was simulating eating along with him. I have saved the video of this for his eighteenth birthday. If that isn't enough of an endorsement, I don't know what is! SERVES 4-6

- 3 ears of corn cobs or 300g (10½oz) frozen sweetcorn
- 300g (10½oz) packet of corn or wheat tortilla wraps
- 3-4 tablespoons oil
- 3 tomatoes, red or green or a mix works, roughly diced
- 2 red onions, finely sliced
- 1 large jar or 2 x 400g (14oz) cans black beans, drained, red kidney or pinto beans also work
- 25g (1oz) coriander, roughly chopped
- juice of 4 limes, plus extra to serve
- 100-200g (3½-7oz) feta (optional)
- sea salt flakes

1. Preheat the oven to 180°C (350°F), Gas Mark 4. Blanch the sweetcorn in salted boiling water for 4-6 minutes until tender. If using frozen, I find pouring 1.5 litres (2⅔ pints) of water over the kernels and letting it stand for 2-3 minutes is enough. Drain and cut the kernels from the cobs when cool enough to handle.

2. In a stack, cut the tortillas into sixths to form little triangles. Toss with the oil and a pinch of salt. Spread evenly and not overlapping on a baking sheet and toast in the oven for 7-10 minutes until crisp and golden. Remove to a wire rack until ready to serve.

3. In a mixing bowl, combine the sweetcorn, tomatoes, onions, beans, coriander and lime juice. Add a good pinch of salt and taste, then add more lime juice if needed. Serve on a platter or bowl with the feta crumbled over if using and the tortilla chips alongside.

BEANS PULSES & SEEDS

Having cooked **BEANS AND PULSES** to hand is so useful to get a nourishing and satisfying meal. Dried beans and pulses in all their forms are things of wonder. They can be used in so many different ways and lend themselves to different cuisines effortlessly. They deserve a deep dive if only for their names: red fox carlin peas, gogmagog, good mother stallard, eye of goat – to name a few from the Hodmedod's website, which is where I get the majority of my dried beans from. I tend to buy in bulk as they keep well. That being said, I always like to keep an arsenal of tins and jars in case preplanning hasn't been on the cards.

CHICKPEA, green pepper & dill salad

I love it when peppers start appearing at the markets as I know we will have loads of really fresh and crunchy salads like this. Between myself and my son, a couple of peppers don't even make it home. I often forget to actually cook with them that much these days. If I'm taking a packed lunch for myself or my son Wilfred, I pack us a whole pepper each. I made this salad for him one lunchtime and it was such a hit we just have it on rotation throughout the season.

SERVES 4 AS A SIDE OR 2 AS A LIGHT LUNCH

- 660g (1lb 7½oz) jar chickpeas, or 2 x 400g (14oz) tins or 330g (11½oz) soaked and cooked dried chickpeas
- 25g (1oz) dill
- 1 small red onion, finely diced
- 250ml (9fl oz) kefir or natural yogurt
- 3 green peppers, about 360g (12½oz)

TO SERVE
- good olive oil
- 1–2 good pinches of pul biber or chilli flakes (optional)

1. Drain the chickpeas, reserving the liquid to make the plant-based mayo on page 12 as it's always worth having a batch made up in the fridge.

2. Add the chickpeas to a large mixing bowl with the dill, onion and kefir.

3. Slice the peppers into 1cm (½in) rounds. Pull out any seeds and stalks and compost. Add to the mixing bowl. Toss everything together. Lay out on a serving dish with a good drizzle of oil and a few pinches of chilli flakes if you like.

LENTIL bolognese

I've never tasted the traditional Bolognese that I make. It's a strange concept making food for people that you can't eat yourself. But I get called on to make my meat version for kids' parties or gatherings and I'm happy cooking behind the hob, plus I pack lots of veg into it. However, I wanted to make a lentil version using essentially the same ratios and technique. Let the vegetables cook down quite a bit so they are really soft and starting to caramelize. For a brighter version, use split red lentils. They will need less cooking time, so are also a good option if you're pushed for time. I save the rinds from hard cheese then drop a couple into the pan with the tomatoes to add an extra layer of flavour. SERVES 6

- 4 tablespoons olive oil
- 2 onions, roughly diced
- 1 fennel bulb, tough stalks removed, diced
- 2 celery sticks, diced
- 2 carrots, tops removed and diced
- 3 garlic cloves
- 2 leeks, trimmed, cleaned and diced
- 2 bay leaves
- 250g (9oz) green or brown lentils, puy work well
- 250ml (8½fl oz) white wine
- 2 x 400g (14oz) cans plum tomatoes
- 500g (1lb 2oz) spaghetti or linguine, but any favoured shape is fine

TO SERVE
- extra-virgin olive oil
- hard Italian-style cheese, grated or blitzed to crumbs in a blender

1. In a pan over a medium heat, add the oil, followed by all the ingredients except for the lentils, wine and tomatoes. Cook for 10–15 minutes until the onions are soft and translucent.

2. Add the lentils and the wine. Then add the tomatoes. Crush them up a bit and add in 2 cans' worth of water. Bring to a simmer and cook for a further 20–25 minutes until the lentils are tender. The sauce wants to be thickened and no longer watery. If it needs longer, keep it going and top up with water accordingly.

3. Cook your pasta according to your taste. When done, drain, reserving a cup or so of pasta water. Add the pasta to the sauce and loosen with the reserved water if needed. Spoon onto plates followed with any sauce left in the pan. Add a drizzle of olive oil and cheese on the side.

YELLOW SPLIT PEAS
with curried ghee, beetroot salsa & yogurt

This is another dish where I enjoy making the base and then take it in different directions depending on what is on hand and how the mood takes me. Raita and crispy onions are good options. Frying eggs in the curried ghee/clarified butter is also delicious. Topped with spring onions, chilli and herbs, this makes for a great breakfast or indeed also works well atop the split peas.

SERVES 8

- 50ml (1¾fl oz) neutral oil, such as groundnut or sunflower
- 3 onions, roughly chopped
- 3 medium carrots, diced
- 1 fennel bulb, diced
- 3 garlic cloves, roughly sliced
- 2 bay leaves
- 500g (1lb 2oz) yellow split peas
- 2 x 400ml (14fl oz) cans coconut milk
- sea salt flakes and black pepper

FOR THE BEETROOT SALSA
- 6 beetroots, the lighter-coloured ones are best: yellow, white or candy-striped, although purple is fine, and carrot also works well
- 1 small red onion, thinly sliced
- juice of 1 lemon
- 1 tablespoon poppy seeds

TO SERVE
- 150g (5½oz) ghee, butter or oil also works
- 1 tablespoon curry powder or 1 tablespoon mix of ground cumin, coriander, turmeric and chilli powder
- natural yogurt
- 3 spring onions, trimmed and sliced
- handful of coriander
- rotis or flatbreads

1. Heat the oil in a good-sized pan. Sauté the onions, carrots, fennel and garlic for 10 minutes until beginning to soften well. Add the bay leaves and cook for a further 5 minutes. Add the split peas and some salt, along with 2 litres (3½ pints) of water and bring to a simmer. Skim any scum that appears on top. Cook for 45 minutes or until the split peas reach the desired texture – I like them to retain a little bite at this stage, as they will be cooked further each time you reheat them. Season to taste with salt and pepper.

2. At this point the split peas are ready and can be used for other meals if desired. Otherwise, carry on and add the coconut milk and cook until the split peas thicken again – you're looking for a thick, soup-like consistency.

3. Grate the beetroot and mix together with the sliced red onion. Squeeze in the lemon juice and add the poppy seeds and it's done.

4. Warm the ghee in a pan until melted. Add the curry powder or mixed spices and heat through until you can smell the aromas. Turn off the heat and set aside for serving – the mix can always be rewarmed gently to melt it again.

5. Divide the split peas between bowls. Top with the beetroot salsa, yogurt, sliced spring onions and coriander, then finally a few spoonfuls of the curried ghee. Eat with rotis or flatbreads.

PEAS & cheese on toast

Great as a breakfast or a light lunch/dinner, I often remember about this dish when I'm doing long stints of work from home. It has both the comfort and nourishment levels to satisfy and energize. Remember to put the peas on to soak when going up to bed, so come the morning they only need a little time on the hob. I tend to make this amount for just myself and reheat portions as I need them. Sprinkling in your favourite vinegar does really lift the flavours. The crispy toast soaking up the juices and getting soggy underneath is like giant crouton. One of those dishes that is relatively simple, is fortifying and brings so much pleasure. SERVES 4

- 2 tablespoons olive oil, plus extra to serve if you like
- 2 onions, roughly diced
- 300g (10½oz) marrowfat peas, soaked overnight
- 1–2 tablespoons cider vinegar, or to taste
- 100g (3½oz) hard cheese, cow's, sheep's or goat's all work
- sea salt flakes and black pepper
- slices of crusty sourdough, toasted, to serve

1. In a pan, heat the oil over a medium heat. Add the onions and cook for 5–7 minutes until fairly soft. Drain and rinse your peas. Place in the pan with plenty of water, bring to the boil, cover and simmer for 40–50 minutes until tender. If the water gets too low, just top it up.

2. Taste to see if the peas are cooked. Add salt and vinegar to your liking.

3. I like to blend hard cheese to the texture of crumbs if I'm using it on hot dishes. It helps the cheese disperse over the food better. It also saves on grating time.

4. Spoon the peas onto the slices of toast and add cheese to your liking. Lots of black pepper cracked over. A drizzle of olive oil if you like.

Silken *TOFU* dressed in Szechuan vinegar sauce

This is my take on a central Asian sauce. I keep a block or two of silken tofu in the cupboard just for this recipe. The creamy tofu works really well with the punchy sauce. Rather than serving the blocks of tofu, you can mix everything together to form a noodle salad. If you have sauce left over, it is good on anything you see fit, with egg fried rice being a favourite of mine. I bash the seeds a bit in the pestle and mortar to keep a coarser texture. SERVES 4

- 1 tablespoon (7g/¼oz) coriander seeds, crushed
- 1 tablespoon (7g/¼oz) cumin seeds, crushed
- 1 tablespoon (7g/¼oz) chilli flakes
- 40ml (1½fl oz) sunflower oil
- 2–3 spring onions, sliced into quarters lengthways, then into small dice
- 80g (2¾oz) tomato purée
- 3–5 tablespoons rice wine vinegar, to taste
- 2 x 300g (10½oz) blocks silken tofu
- 200g (7oz) pack of noodles, cooked, I use flat brown rice noodles, but do use your favourite kind of rice noodle (or see page 95 for homemade)

FOR THE SALAD
- ½ cucumber, cut into thin batons
- ¼–½ white cabbage, shredded
- handful of mint leaves
- handful of coriander leaves
- 2–3 spring onions, finely sliced
- 3 tablespoons toasted sesame seeds
- 1 red chilli, finely sliced

1. In a small saucepan over a medium heat, toast the coriander and cumin seeds and chilli flakes until aromatic. A minute or so should do. Remove and set aside. Add the oil and spring onions. Mix well to combine, then cook for 1–2 minutes. Then follow with the tomato purée. Cook this out for a further minute, then add the spices back in and rice wine vinegar to taste. You will most likely need to let the sauce down with a little water until it becomes a spooning consistency. It wants to be saucy but not too loose.

2. Mix the salad ingredients together and arrange on a serving plate. Spoon the sauce over the tofu on individual plates or a serving dish. Serve the noodles alongside. Or mix everything together to form a noodle salad.

Spiced
CHICKPEA pastilla

I love these crispy, flaky parcels filled with moreish spiced chickpeas. A great light lunch or wonderful to take along on picnics, or even put in the kids' packed lunches. I've taken influences for this dish from trips to Morocco. I always felt left out when everyone was having pigeon pastilla, so wanted to create a Moroccan-inspired vegetarian version. MAKES 12

- 6 tablespoons olive oil
- 3 onions, halved and sliced, from root to tip
- 3 courgettes (about 500g/1lb 2oz)
- 3 fat garlic cloves, sliced
- 1 heaped tablespoon ras el hanout
- 660g (1lb 7½oz) jar chickpeas, drained, 2 x 400g (14oz) tins drained also work
- 250g (9oz) filo pastry (12 sheets)
- 1 tablespoon cumin seeds
- 1 tablespoon ground cinnamon
- sea salt flakes

FOR THE CRUNCHY YOGURT SALAD
- 2 kohlrabi, peeled, or 1 cucumber or 1 fennel bulb, or a mix, finely diced
- 1 red onion, finely diced
- 25g (1oz) dill, finely chopped
- 2 tablespoons white wine vinegar
- 8 tablespoons natural yogurt
- 2 tablespoons extra-virgin olive oil

1. In a medium pan over a medium heat, add 3 tablespoons of oil and the onions with a good pinch of salt. Cook for 10–15 minutes until soft and beginning to colour, stirring fairly often.

2. Meanwhile, slice the courgettes into quarters lengthways. Then run a small knife along the length to remove the inner soft part and compost. Halve these sections along their lengths and cut down them to form cubes roughly the size of the chickpeas. Then add to the onions when they are beginning to caramelize, along with the garlic. Cook for a further 10–12 minutes until the courgettes are soft.

3. Add the ras el hanout, give it a good stir and cook for a minute. Add the chickpeas, cook for a further minute and then turn off the heat. Check the seasoning and adjust accordingly.

4. Combine the yogurt salad ingredients and set aside. Preheat the oven to 180°C (350°F), Gas Mark 4. Lightly oil two baking sheets.

5. Lay out a sheet of filo. Then, with the remaining oil, lightly brush along one long edge. Fold the sheet in half to seal so you have a long rectangle. Spoon a twelfth of the chickpea mix onto the top right corner, tucked up toward the top into the corner but leaving a 1cm (½in) gap from the edge. Arrange the mixture into a rough triangle, then bring the corner down to meet the bottom edge of the pastry near you. I like to gently press and arrange the mixture inside to get it as evenly distributed as possible. Keep folding the parcel down the length of the pastry until you have a neat triangle.

6. Place on a baking sheet. Repeat with the remaining chickpea mixture and filo pastry. Brush each parcel evenly with oil, then sprinkle on the cumin seeds and a pinch of sea salt flakes. Bake for 30–40 minutes, rotating the baking sheets after 20 minutes. Lightly dust with the cinnamon and serve with the salad.

RED LENTIL
coconut curry

Very much a go-to that everyone enjoys, this can happily be eaten as a soup or more of a curry paired with rice or grains. Fresh, crunchy toppings play well against the warming comfort of the lentils. I mostly don't bother peeling ginger these days, as long as it is clean enough and washed thoroughly. I just grate it and most of the skin stays behind anyway. If you do peel it, use a teaspoon to scrape away the skin. SERVES 4

- 3 tablespoons oil, I use sunflower
- 2 red onions, roughly diced
- 4 garlic cloves
- 50–60g (1¾– 2¼oz) ginger, washed and finely grated
- 4 lemongrass stalks, soft centres removed and finely sliced, keep the outer stalks
- 400g (14oz) can plum tomatoes
- 400ml (14fl oz) can coconut milk
- 250g (9oz) split red lentils
- sea salt flakes

TO SERVE *(optional)*
- white cabbage, shredded
- cucumber, sliced or cut into a dice
- chilli, sliced or cut into a dice
- spring onion, sliced or cut into a dice
- mint, leaves picked
- coriander, leaves picked
- natural yogurt

1. In a saucepan that will fit everything, heat the oil over a medium heat. Add the onions and cook for 5–7 minutes. Follow with the garlic, ginger and lemongrass. Cook for another 3–5 minutes. I like to add the lemongrass stalks so they can impart their flavour as well. Just remember to fish them out later. Tying them together with string helps with this.

2. Add the tomatoes and roughly break them up with your stirring spoon. Add the coconut milk and a full can's worth of water. Add the lentils and a good pinch of salt. Bring to a simmer and cook for 10–15 minutes until the lentils are soft.

3. Check the seasoning and add more salt if needed. Serve with whichever garnish you like alongside.

Spiced *BLACK BADGERS*

Black badgers are also known as brown carlin peas or black/grey peas. They have wonderful markings. You can use whatever peas or beans you like in this. It is just a rough template of a recipe that I make most weeks, with or without the peppers. Try other spices to take it in different directions. It goes well with rice or other grains, or just eaten as it is with some yogurt and herbs on top. SERVES 4 OR 8 IF SERVED WITH RICE OR GRAINS

- 300g (10½oz) black badgers or dried beans of your choice, soaked overnight
- 3 tablespoons olive oil
- 2 onions, diced
- 2 carrots, tops removed, diced
- 2 peppers, stalks and most of the seeds removed, diced
- 2 x 400g (14oz) cans plum tomatoes
- 1 teaspoon ground coriander
- 1 teaspoon cumin, ground, or seeds, crushed
- 1 teaspoon paprika, sweet or hot or a blend
- sea salt flakes

TO SERVE
- natural yogurt
- few handfuls of herbs
- pickled chillies (see page 90 for homemade)

1. Drain and rinse your peas. Add them to a pan with plenty of water. Bring to the boil, cover and simmer for 40–50 minutes until tender.

2. Meanwhile, in another pan over a medium heat, add the oil, followed by the onions, carrots and a good pinch of salt. Cook for 10–12 minutes until the onions are soft and translucent. Add the peppers and tomatoes and spices. Break up the tomatoes a little and bring to a simmer. Let it bubble away for 10 minutes.

3. Drain the beans and add to the sauce. Cook together for 5–10 minutes, check the seasoning and then either serve straight away or leave off the heat to let the flavours marry further as they will improve with time. Serve with the yogurt, herbs and pickled chillies alongside.

DAL MAKHANI

When visiting our friend Henrietta Inman who runs the fantastic Wakelyns Bakery in Suffolk, we had this amazing dal makhani made by Lakshmi Yuvaraj, who makes food at the Wholefood Store and Café in Manningtree. It tasted out of this world good, while being deeply familiar and comforting. There is a little tickle of spice that comes in at the end riding over the richness. Just brilliant. Henri paired this with grains from Hodmedod's and piles of crunchy, fresh salad with green and yellow beans. We sat outside and ate what I consider to be a perfect plate of food. This for me is it. This is Lakshmi's recipe; I can't claim any credit. The pairing is Henri's. I just put it down here so everyone can recreate it. When I make this recipe and eat it, I spend the whole time smiling. Lakshmi says that it will last for a month in the fridge. The high fat content preserves everything. If in rush or you forget to soak the lentils, you can just cook them straight. I have done this before; the lentils will just hold their shape more. SERVES 8

- 500g (1lb 2oz) 5 olive green, speckled lentils
- 2 tablespoons ghee
- 3 garlic cloves, finely grated
- thumb of fresh root ginger, washed and finely grated
- 1 tablespoon Kashmiri chilli powder
- 2 x 400g (14oz) cans plum tomatoes
- 250g (9oz) unsalted butter, roughly diced
- 250ml (9fl oz) double cream
- grains of your choice, to serve

FOR THE SALAD
- a mix of some or all of the following: a few handfuls of cabbage, cavolo nero or salad leaves
- thinly sliced raw courgettes, fennel and/or spring onions
- fresh or blanched peas and/or fine beans
- lots of herbs
- pinch of salt
- lemon juice, to taste

1. Rinse the lentils and soak overnight. Add the lentils to a pan with 1.5 litres (2⅔ pints) of water. Bring to a simmer and cook for about 20–25 minutes until tender.

2. In a large pan or wok over a medium heat, add the ghee followed by the garlic and ginger. Cook for 1–2 minutes until the raw smell goes. Now add the chilli powder. Stir it in quickly and follow with the lentils. Stir well to combine and then add the tomatoes. I crush them up with my wooden spoon when they are in the pan. Cook, stirring often, until the tomatoes and lentils begin to stick to the bottom of the pan. Be careful as it can start to spit.

3. Reduce the heat to medium–low and add the butter. Continue to cook gently and keep on stirring. Let it bubble away gently for 15–20 minutes.

4. Assemble the salad ingredients and mix together with the salt and lemon juice to taste.

5. Add the cream to the dal and cook for 5 minutes. Serve with the salad and grains of your choice. Or cool and keep in the fridge until ready to reheat.

HERB & cashew cream dip

Whether you have a high-speed blender or not dictates whether you soak the cashews. If it isn't high speed, then 2–3 hours of soaking will help the cashews break down more easily. You could also use this as a plant-based sauce for pasta or noodles. Or to use in place of yogurt for topping soups and stews. MAKES 750G (1LB 10OZ)

- 300g (10½oz) cashews (soaking optional, see intro)
- 400ml (14fl oz) water
- 4 spring onions
- juice of ½ lemon, plus extra to taste
- 25g (1oz) coriander
- 25g (1oz) mint, leaves picked
- sea salt flakes

TO DIP (optional)
- cucumber, sliced
- cherry tomatoes
- carrots, sliced
- radishes, sliced
- peppers, sliced
- little gem lettuce, sliced
- crisps

1. Add the ingredients to a blender with a good pinch of salt and blitz on high until very smooth. Check the seasoning and lemon levels and add more if needed. Serve with your favourite things to dip.

CHICKPEAS in tomato pulp dressing, thick yogurt & marjoram

A really simple showcase of ingredients, which is a handy dish to have up your sleeve. Generally, I tend to have all the ingredients in, especially in the summer when tomatoes are in season. As well as being really easy to pull together, it is great as a quick light lunch or as a side, or even a starter at a dinner party. Herb-wise basil or other soft herbs work just fine. We have a marjoram plant, so I tend to grab a handful from that.

SERVES 4 AS A SIDE

- 300g (10½oz) really ripe and flavourful tomatoes
- juice of 1 lemon (about 60ml/2¼fl oz)
- 3 tablespoons extra-virgin olive oil, plus extra for drizzling
- handful of marjoram, leaves picked and roughly chopped
- 660g (1lb 7½oz) jar chickpeas, drained, or 330g (11½oz) soaked and cooked dried chickpeas
- 250g (9oz) natural yogurt
- sea salt flakes and black pepper

1. Grate the tomatoes on a coarse box grater or over a mixing bowl. To start them off, I begin working in a circular motion until the skin breaks. Compost the stalks.

2. Add the lemon juice, oil and marjoram to the bowl, followed by the chickpeas. Mix well and taste for salt levels. Jarred chickpeas can be pretty well salted already, so be judicious initially.

3. Spread the yogurt out on a serving dish. Top with the chickpeas and a final drizzle of oil. Crack over a good amount of black pepper.

index